Advance

Review

Copy

# PLAYING THE GAME

Turning My Personal Defeat
into Aviation History

A Memoir

David D. Strachan

Edited with an Introduction by Brenda Carpenter Osayim

Published by David D. Strachan
Information available at playingthegame.memoir@gmail.com
Cover art by David D. Strachan & Brenda Carpenter Osayim
Book design by D. Bass

ISBN: 978-0-9967595-0-2

*This book is dedicated with love to the memory*
*of my parents,*
*Jonathan D. Strachan and Annie Donaldson Strachan*

COVER PHOTO: 1LT David D. Strachan, U.S. Air Force, 313th Air Divison, HQ, Okinawa, Japan, 1957

# Contents

# Introduction

Almost a century ago, the poet Langston Hughes asked, *"What happens to a dream deferred?"* For David D. Strachan, the answer to this question has been a lifetime's pursuit.

Born and raised in Harlem, New York, David D. Strachan joined the Air Force in 1956 after graduating from New York University and, almost immediately, was "washed out" of pilot training because of the color of his skin. He was devastated and his dream of becoming a pilot was all but destroyed, but David's anger and frustration did not "fester like a sore," in the words of the poet; nor did it "explode." Instead, through means that become painfully clear as he tells the story of his own personal tragedies, he was able to rise like the phoenix and reinvent his purpose in life. His definition of success became accomplishment, not necessarily for himself, but for hundreds of young African American and Latino men and women whom he was able to influence as a mentor.

The recipient of more certificates and awards than he can remember, David earned the title *Teacher of the Year* from Brooklyn District Attorney, Charles Hynes, while teaching at Wingate High School in Brooklyn, New York and has twice been designated an *Outstanding Teacher* by St. Francis College, also in Brooklyn. So many of his Wingate High School students attended flight training in Ozark, Alabama that he was once awarded the *Key to the City* in recognition of his contribution to the local economy. In 1999, he was named an *Honoree* of the International Forest of Friendship in Atchinson, Kansas. Of the numerous accolades Mr. Strachan has received during his lifetime, none is as revealing as a plaque presented to him by one of his former students. It reads, "*You are the wind beneath my wings.*"

In reading the success stories of the men and women in this book, one cannot help but wonder what would happen to educational and criminal statistics in this country if every single child, black and white, Latino and Asian and Native Peoples, were empowered to follow their dream. Many black men and women turn their anger and frustration inward, blaming themselves for their economic failure and drowning themselves in alcoholism, drug abuse, gun violence and other forms of self-destruction, aided and abetted by genuinely barbarian law enforcement officials and a health care system that reeks of apartheid. This model has become the *status quo* and it works wonderfully to the advantage of European-descendent Americans, citizens and non-citizens alike. David D. Strachan has turned this paradigm on its head. The attempt to prevent him from fully participating in the American Dream backfired: instead of engaging in self-destruction, David D. Strachan *got even*.

Though this story is built on memories, its scope far exceeds that of an ordinary memoir. In the author's own words, "This memoir includes the stories of the Everest-like climb of some poor black students in a Brooklyn, New York ghetto high school. This was accomplished here in America where white-supremacy racism is still in effect and drove many of them to the captain's seat as professional pilots. How was this done? Read this book and you will meet young people who were able to leap forward, educationally and economically, while also reaching back to help others behind them as they took their own achievements to greater heights." As one of the pilots interviewed for this project pointed out, "We're not in jail, we're not on welfare; we're supporting ourselves and our families, and we're doing everything the opposite of what they said we were supposed to be doing."

*Playing the Game* fills a massive void. It can be read as a step-by-step instructional manual on how to become a pilot, information that any high school guidance counselor *should* have at his/her fingertips. Long overdue, it serves equally well as a handbook for survival for young people of color who wish to follow their professional aspirations in a world still not able to accept them/us as valid individuals with real hopes and real dreams. The advice contained herein should help black people everywhere deal effectively with the institution of white supremacy. There is a "race" issue here, whether we admit it or not, and on a social and economic level, sooner or later this country is going to have to deal with this issue.

Not every episode in the history of African American aviation is included in this memoir. There is mention, several times, of the legendary Tuskegee Airmen and their equally legendary instructor, "Chief" Charles Alfred Anderson who, in the absence of a white instructor who would agree to teach him how to fly, taught himself. Bessie Coleman is mentioned, as is Marlon Green, the first black American to sue a commercial carrier because of discriminatory hiring practices, and Ruth Carol Taylor, the first black flight attendant. Many others are omitted, partly because their encounters with aviation were not contemporaneous with David D. Strachan's story. World War I flying ace Eugene Bullard, sometimes referred to as "The Father of African American Aviation," is one of those. Like any memoir, there are limitations to the scope of history that can be included in one volume.

There are also a significant number of personal stories that had to be pared down during the editing process. Each of the Wingate pilots could write his/her own memoir recounting their singular journey to success, regardless of their chosen field, for each and every one of them has a fascinating story to tell. Dozens of intriguing anecdotes had to be omitted from the narrative in order to preserve the focus of David D. Strachan's own urgent message.

Audre Lorde, Poet Laureate of New York State at the time of her untimely death, once wrote, *"We were never meant to survive."* This book is David D. Strachan's response to her searing observation. David D. Strachan has been accused many times in his life of being a racist, but his students and those who know him well call him a *game-changer*. There should be no doubt: this memoir will be a game-changer for future generations.

Brenda Carpenter Osayim
September 2015

# PLAYING

# THE

# GAME

Part I: *My Personal Defeat*

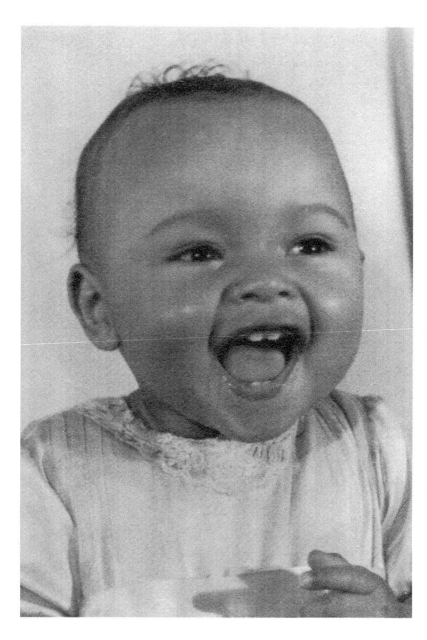

David D. Strachan as an infant

# Chapter One:
## *You Can't Get There From Here*

My name is David D. Strachan and I was born on 28 August 1933. The "D" stands for Donaldson, which was my mother's maiden name. My mother, Annie Donaldson Strachan, was called "Ma." She was a beautiful, dark, brown-skinned woman who was full-figured but never fat. Mother was born in Jamaica in the latter part of the 19th century. Daddy, as we called my father Jonathan, was also born in Jamaica in the 19th century. They both came to the United States in the early part of the 20th century. Both of them spoke the "King's English" with no traces of Jamaican patois in their speech. Curse words or slang never came across their lips.

Daddy was an extremely handsome man who always wore a shirt and tie with a jacket or suit, along with a Fedora hat. I never saw him in a cap. He worked as a clerk at the post office, one of the best jobs available to a black man during the Great Depression. When he went to his job, he carried his lunch in a briefcase, never in a bag or lunchbox.

My father "brought home the bacon" in the form of U.S. dollars. My mother rented three apartments at 281 Edgecombe Avenue in Harlem, New York, and leased rooms to individuals and families for as little as five dollars per week, including linen service. My father was able to buy a number of pieces of real estate, including a tenement building on 114th St. in Harlem and some brownstones in Brooklyn.

We lived in Apt. 1-F, one of the top floor apartments that my mother rented, and always had a male roomer in our apartment. My mother's younger sister, Ethel Donaldson, also lived with us. Ethel was, as we called her, a spinster. She worked as a domestic for a while and then moved on to become a garment worker and

Annie Donaldson Strachan and Jonathan D. Strachan in the 1920s. The inscription in the lower right reads, "Compliments of Mr. & Mrs. J.D. Strachan." Photo courtesy of Edward A. Strachan.

Uncle Charlie          Aunt Ethel in the 1920s

a member of the International Ladies' Garment Workers Union.

Apt. 1-F was a big apartment with a long hallway that had two bedrooms, one for my mother's sister, Ethel, and one for the male roomer. My parents had a bedroom facing the street and Colonial Park (now called Jackie Robinson Park), which was across the street from our building. My brother Ed and I also shared a room facing the park. We ate in the kitchen, but we had another room that we used as a dining room at times. The bathroom was in the long hallway facing the courtyard.

We had family members, aunts and uncles, living in the same building and throughout the neighborhood. My favorite person was my father's sister, Aunt Lil, who lived on the fourth floor with Uncle Charlie, who owned a tailor shop. Aunt Lil held court with Uncle Charlie every Sunday afternoon for our Jamaican family and friends. I made sure to end up at her place on Sundays for my second dinner, after eating at home. Aunt Lil worked in the garment industry, also. I remember her doing what was called "homework." This was work handed out by the factory owner for workers to take home and complete.

Aunt Lil also sold Avon cosmetics. She purchased far more products than she could sell. When she died, she left what looked like a half-ton of unsold Avon products in her apartment. For much of the time Aunt Lil lived at 281 Edgecombe Avenue, she had only an icebox, rather than a refrigerator, which required her to buy ice from the iceman like most people at that time. My mother and father had a refrigerator. I've never lived in an apartment without a refrigerator, even though many of the people around where we lived did not have one. Most people had no telephone. My family had a telephone that we let people on our floor use.

Mother cooked all the meals, maintained the apartment, and kept up her room-rental business in our three apartments. On Sunday mornings in the 1930s and 40s, she would serve a breakfast of bacon and eggs with rolls made by Mrs. Brown, a neighbor who lived on the second floor who sold them. We ate, using lots of but-

Jonathan and Edward in front of the entrance to 281 Edgecombe Avenue

Jonathan and Annie
Donaldson Strachan, Easter
Sunday, 1954

Annie D. Strachan (l.),
Aunt Ethel (c.), and a
neighbor, Easter, 1954

ter at that time. None of us ever heard of "cholesterol."

I would go places with my mother and ride on the trolley cars of the day or the elevated train – we used to call it the "El" – that ran along Eighth Avenue, which is now called Frederick Douglass Boulevard. Eighth Avenue was lined with pushcarts and people selling produce. The subways cost only a nickel in 1936. My mother paid the fare for many people.

It was in the middle of autumn in 1936 when my mother, Annie Donaldson Strachan, came home from New York/Columbia Medical Center with my new brother, Edward, born 4 October 1936. I told her after seeing him that she could take him back to the place where she got him.

That same year, my father, with some of his friends, sailed to Germany to attend the Olympic games in Berlin. He was there for Jesse Owen's victory. Many years later, my oldest daughter Davia came home and informed me that her teacher told her that she was lying when she said that her grandfather had attended the 1936 Olympic games. I showed up at the school the next day with photos of his attendance at those games. My daughter was very pleased that I could back her with those photos.

My mother was always home for me and my brother. I never heard her or my father talk badly about anyone, not even those who did them wrong in their lives. They gave my younger brother and myself wonderful loving care. The truth is that we were over-nourished to a condition of being overweight, or obese, during part of my childhood years. People would say that we looked prosperous; at that time, the state of being fat was equated with prosperity.

Living at 281 Edgecombe Avenue in Harlem, in our apartment overlooking Colonial Park with my mother, Annie, and father, Jonathan, was a pleasure each and every day. During the summer, my father took me and my brother to the swimming pool at Colonial Park and we learned to be excellent swimmers. We went to many sporting events with my father. Track and field was the sport that I enjoyed the most. We got to go to all the big track meets at Mad-

David D. Strachan and his brother Edward growing up in Harlem. Above left: Toddlers in the 1930s. Above right: c.1940. Below left: The 1940s. Below right: On the roof at 281 Edgecombe Avenue, Easter Monday, 1954.

ison Square Garden, which in those days was located on Eighth Avenue at 54th St. I noticed in those days that most of the black athletes were in the sprints, that is to say, the short races. Some people used to say that black folks were not capable of competing in the mile or other long races. Things have certainly changed.

During the baseball season, we would go to the Negro League games at Yankee Stadium or the Polo Grounds. I attended the 1939 World's Fair with my father, Jonathan, who was a great role model in my life. He was able to send me to college without having to take out any college loans for me to repay.

At the end of the 1930s and in the early 40s, I recall seeing lots of men hollering along Eighth Avenue and other places like that. My mother told me that they were "shell shocked." I guess today you would call that post-traumatic stress disorder. They were veterans from the First World War.

My father had been married once before he married my mother. My two brothers from that union were named James (whom we called Jim) and John. They would visit with us from time to time. Jim was an extremely handsome man who became a New York City firefighter; John was a postal clerk who was appointed as one of the first black postmasters for New York City by President Lyndon B. Johnson. In addition, both of them were musicians: John played the saxophone and Jim played the trumpet. John was a soldier in the Second World War whose job it was to play in the Army Band. Both of them have long-since passed on, John from a brain tumor and Jim from ALS, or Lou Gehrig's Disease. They both graduated from college as adults and eventually earned master's degrees.

Women must have liked my father, who died in 1966. I remember a man coming up to me when I was living in the Bronx, sometime around 1970, and telling me that my father was also his father. He disappeared and I never saw him again.

James A. Strachan, 1933

John R. Strachan, 1933

F.F.C. James A. Strachan (1915-1989), FDNY Engine Company 24, Manhattan (1939-1959). James was also the co-founder and first elected vice-president of the Vulcan Society (1940).

John R. Strachan, 1963. John was a career employee with the Postal Service and was one of the first black men in the U.S. to be appointed to the position of Postmaster.

I remember the 1939 World's Fair, when I got to ride in a Ford automobile that was on display. I started first grade at P.S.186 on 145th St. in Manhattan that same year. P.S.186 was a building shaped in the form of an "H," with primary grades only. When I got there in 1939, there were lots of white children. By the time I graduated from sixth grade, most of them had disappeared.

I loved girls at an early age. June Cunningham and Alma Craft were my favorites: never will I forget them and I wonder where they are now. What happened to Mary Davis and Rita Schiff, whose father was a veterinarian on 145th St. near Amsterdam Avenue?

All of my teachers were white. I never had a regular black teacher from the first to the twelfth grade in the schools here in New York City (sometimes there were black substitutes, but that was rare). I was never taught to be a writer, from first to twelfth grades. One English teacher at George Washington High School called my writing "ignorant." This stifled me in regard to writing; it took me a very long time to overcome this shutting down.

Never once in the New York City schools did I see or read a book written by a black person. The only literature we read was authored by dead European males. It took me a long time to overcome the damage done to me in school, including the block I had against writing. I feel now that the Board of Education should have been sued for malfeasance.

George Washington High School was a large school with thousands of students in the Washington Heights section of New York. The curriculum consisted of three different tracks: I was in Track 1, called academic. Track 2 was called commercial and Track 3 was called general. To my recollection, most of the black students were clustered in the general track.

Mr. Kutcher was my mathematics teacher in twelfth grade. Math teacher Kutcher was a short, fat man full of racism. He was known by some students as "Kutcher the Butcher." He was also a cruel person who told another black student in the math class that

Young David in front of *The Harp*, a sculpture by Augusta Savage
at the 1939 World's Fair.

he was not "sitting on a banana tree eating bananas" on the Caribbean island from which he came. He did not like me and decided to give me a failing grade that I did not deserve. However, my father was having none of this. He went to the school and made the principal correct the grade to passing, which was what I deserved.

In all the years from first grade to the twelfth, I cannot remember even one teacher saying anything empowering to me in terms of going ahead in my life. The secret of being a great teacher is to love your students. If you have this love, you as a teacher will be inspired to do what is required to bring them to excellence. George Washington High School was a place where I did not develop any affinity. It was a large building, sitting by itself on the top of a hill, that I was glad to leave and hoped never to return to. With one exception, I never had any contact with anyone connected to the school after graduation. I did have occasion to visit the school, once, years later as an auditor.

After leaving George Washington High School, I attended New York University (NYU). My father paid the full tuition, enabling me to get an education without having a ball-and-chain, *i.e.*, student loans, attached to me when I graduated. It was nice to attend school at the Washington Square campus, but I was struggling with classes. I knew then and I still know now that the weak foundation I received from kindergarten through twelfth grades was against me. However, I managed to pass all my classes with low grades. I was able to stay on at NYU and even thrive after getting help with my writing from a friend. A woman professor, an instructor of English, did not believe that I had written the work I turned in.

I enrolled in the Reserve Officer Training Corps (ROTC) at NYU. After four years, in January of 1956, I was able to graduate with teaching credentials in health and physical education. I was commissioned as a second lieutenant in the Air Force, took the test to become a pilot, passed it, and was scheduled to report for orientation at Lackland Air Force Base (AFB) in San Antonio,

Portraits of David D. Strachan (top to bottom, left to right): high school graduation; Eagle Scout; lifeguard at John Jay Pool, 1950; NYU student, 1954.

Texas.

One of the instructors in the ROTC program was a graduate of the Tuskegee experiment to train black pilots during the Second World War. He shot down a number of German planes during the war. I went to him one day requesting guidance on how to jump-start my career as a pilot. His response was, "The Air Force will teach you." I took his word at face value and imagined the training that was ahead for me. I didn't understand at the time that that was a total brush off because there were many things I needed to know in advance about becoming a pilot in the Air Force. My experience with him has demonstrated to me that, even someone who is a survivor of the racist experience of black men in the military, and especially the pilot-training experiment at Tuskegee, could still be uninterested in nurturing another black man following in his footsteps. I trusted him and believed his words. Big mistake. I did not understand how the system of white supremacy in the United States could damage its chief victims, black people, to the point where some of them would not throw a lifeline to those behind them. I had to learn the hard way about the workings of white supremacy in America.

৯৯৯৯

I had orders to report to Lackland AFB on 26 May 1956. My trip down to Texas was the first time I'd ever flown on an airliner, and my arrival in San Antonio was my initiation into Jim Crow segregation. On arrival, I went to a hotel with the expectation of getting a room for the night before reporting for duty the next day. The room clerk explained to me that this hotel was for white people only. Standing there in my new Air Force uniform, ready to protect and defend my country, I listened as he explained that there was a "colored" hotel somewhere in town, but he didn't know where it was. I managed to get a room at the guesthouse on base for the night. During orientation, I was always the only black second lieu-

Air Force ROTC Commissioning Ceremony, February 1956. Front and center is Colonel Andrew F. Gordon. 2LT Strachan stands directly behind Col. Gordon.

Joyce S. Henry and David D. Strachan, wedding ceremony, May 26, 1956.

Lieutenant Strachan departs for Lackland AFB, LaGuardia Airport, June 1956. Seeing him off are his mother, Annie Donaldson Strachan, and brother Edward.

tenant in classes with at least one hundred white lieutenants, and I played the role of *The Invisible Man*.

After a few weeks of orientation at Lackland, I was assigned to a pilot training base called Bainbridge Air Base in southern Georgia. This was July of 1956. This was supposed to be the first step in becoming an Air Force pilot. Friendly faces were in short supply for me at this base, and in this small Georgia town. I heard only a few friendly words from a handful of white student pilots while I was there.

I had gotten married before going into the Air Force at the age of 22, to Joyce Henry, who was 21 and who had graduated as a pharmacist from Fordham University. She was a bright, beautiful black woman who joined me before I reported to the air base in Georgia. We rented a room in the home of a black woman, Mother Beulah, a senior living in the segregated town of Bainbridge. Joyce kept house and I drove to the base each day for "training."

The Air Force ROTC program at NYU in 1955 did not include any flight training. At Air Force pilot training school, I felt like a person who was starting on page one along with other students who were on page one thousand. Many of the students already had aeronautical experience before coming into the Air Force. Nevertheless, I was able to hold my own in the ground school portion of the training.

Half the day was spent in classrooms and the other half was spent at the flight line for flight training with one instructor assigned to teach each of us individually. The instructors at the base were civilians who were contracted by the Air Force. My instructor was a fat white man who, whether purposely or inadvertently, stunted my training. He took me up on my first "instructional flight" and, instead of giving the lesson for a new student, spent my lesson time doing aerobatics. He seemed to be setting me up for failure because every moment of time a student spends in the air is charged to that student. It put me behind before I even started. During my time at the base, I never had even one conversation with another student about flight training. I was completely isolated.

Even with the stress I was under at the base, I was able to learn well enough to have this instructor solo me in a T-34 aircraft, the complex aircraft that I was being trained to fly. In other words, I was able to fly it by myself. After my lessons with him, I was given another instructor for more "lessons" and he then turned me over to the head instructor for evaluation. As I was returning to the airport during this evaluation, I went through my checklist and entered the airport traffic pattern. The runway I was supposed to land on was a parallel runway. I made the mistake of over-flying the right-hand runway, which was the one I was supposed to land on. The head instructor yanked the controls away from me and flew past the right-hand runway over to the left parallel runway and landed the aircraft. He told me that flying was not for me and that I would kill myself. His words felt like daggers to my body and were near-fatal wounds to my self-confidence.

I did not know at the time that over-flying a parallel runway is a common mistake new pilots make. An instructor can easily prompt a student and correct this error. An instructor who is interested in a student's success would not use this mistake to excoriate his student as a failure. It took me many years to recover from this blow to my self-esteem. I could not talk about it for a long time. I had to learn that that kind of mistake was common for students, that even experienced commercial airline pilots have landed on the wrong runway or even at the wrong airport. I feel that those white men were happy to get rid of the only black student pilot at the base. They put me in a coffin, so to speak, but I was not dead yet.

American-style white supremacy was in effect all over Georgia, no matter where you went. One day, Joyce, Mother Beulah and I decided to go to a local drive-in theater (it was really my idea). We got there and I paid for the tickets and was told I could park in the back row of the drive-in. I paid no attention to these instructions and instead, drove to the first row of the theater and we began to watch the movie. Before long, a little white man got out of an old, broken-down truck and brought the manager, who told me I had to leave. I did not argue because I knew how dangerous it was to do that.

Joyce and I went to the base together, once, to use the swimming pool at the Officers' Club. When we appeared at the pool, the officers and their families were not pleased. They said nothing, but looked at me, at the two us, like we were two rats wanting to swim in "their pool," not the base pool. There were no friendly faces. All the white people got out of the water when we went in. We took our short swim and left. We never returned to the Officers' Club pool.

Bainbridge was a miserable place to be. It was totally segregated by American-style Jim Crow, with blacks occupying a place of subjugation enforced by the police. Everyday I saw gangs of African American men chained together like slaves, going out to labor on the roads. This was very common in the state of Georgia in 1956. Once, I needed new license plates, or a "tag" as they call it there, on my car, a 1954 blue Plymouth sedan. To buy the new tag, I had to go to the Bainbridge sheriff's office. In the building where the sheriff's office was located, I passed a water cooler that said, "White People Only," and another nearby that had a sign with the word, "Colored." The one that blacks were supposed to drink from was not a water cooler, but just a spigot. After entering the sheriff's office, I approached the counter and told the man behind it why I was there. He processed my request for the license plate, however, he also reprimanded me for not saying "Yes, sir" to him and told me directly that I had to say "Yes, sir" because he was a white man. I never said it and I was able to walk out without doing what I was told to do. I think he thought I was a *crazy* Negro. In hindsight, my demeanor could have landed me on a tour with a chain gang, or worse.

After being dropped from the pilot training program at Bainbridge Air Base, it took me a long time to realize what I was up against. I didn't know that many, *many* of the students in my classes there had extensive experience in aviation before they even got to the school. Many of them were pilots already. Many of them came from families with pilots and even had their own airplanes. I had gotten into something and I didn't know what I was getting into. Much later on, it reminded me of a saying from Ghana that applied to my condition: *When a fool learns the game, the players have dispersed.* That Ashanti saying has stayed with me throughout my life. It is one of the chief lessons I've repeated to all of my own students. You have to know what's going on before you get into something and I did not have that knowledge. I actually believed what the instructor at NYU told me when he said, "The Air Force will teach you." It does not work like that. If you don't have some training before you get there, you're behind before you even begin, and that is what happened to me.

Somewhere around August of 1956, I was transferred to Tyndall AFB in Panama City, Florida to be trained as a weapons director, that is to say, an officer who guides the pilots by use of radar in the shooting down of enemy aircraft, especially fighter aircraft and bombers. During my training at Tyndall AFB, I lived in the black community with my wife, Joyce, in a small house that we rented next to a railroad track. It was interesting to note that after a while I did not notice the trains that went by; they were not a problem for us. We were isolated with the exception of one black officer friend from base who would stop by at times. I felt terrible going through a training program that I did not want to be in and doing what I did not want to do. I was depressed and, as a result of this feeling, internalized the blame for being eliminated from the pilot training program. I felt like what the bull leaves behind. To soothe my pain, I began to eat and drink too much. Jack Daniels was my favorite.

After completing the radar training, I was assigned to the 313th Air Division in Okinawa, Japan. Okinawa at the time was still under U.S. administration, rather than having been returned to the Japanese government after WWII. Joyce and I drove our Plymouth sedan from Florida to San Francisco, with stops along the way including the Grand Canyon. We had an incident at the top of the canyon in which we got stuck in the snow and got help from a ranger, a white man, who helped us with his driving skills.

Joyce and I made it safely to San Francisco where I was scheduled to catch my deployment flight to Okinawa for the one-year tour of duty. We sold the blue sedan and Joyce flew back to New York alone where she lived with my parents, John and Annie, at 281 Edgecombe Avenue. She worked as a pharmacist and took courses in Spanish at City College. We wrote to each other everyday.

My flight from the U.S. left from Oakland Air Base with stops in Hawaii, Wake Island and Tokyo before reaching Naha, the capital of Okinawa. Tokyo was my introduction to Japanese-style racism. After dinner on the base, I went with four other lieutenants, all of them white, to a club to have a drink. The policy of this Japanese club was to have a hostess sit with each male patron. It did not take but a few moments for me to realize that I was an unwelcome patron. Each of the other lieutenants had a hostess sitting with him. The message to me was that the tentacles of American-style white supremacy had infected Japan and the Japanese people. Subsequent talks with other black military personnel confirmed my observations to be true about supremacist behavior in some Japanese people toward African Americans at that time.

I was assigned to Okino Radar Station, located on a small island called Okinoerabujima, which was under Japanese administration. This Air Force outpost had only about 125 personnel (more or less), including half a dozen officers, which included me. We also had four or five civilian American contractors who were allowed the privilege of living in the officers' quarters with us. There was a major in command of the station, a captain, and maybe four lieutenants. I can remember some of the names of personnel including Lieutenant Steven R. Easton and Lieutenant James E. Durham. A lot of the other people, I can't remember their names. I spent a year at this remote site in rural Japan. This was nothing like living on Okinawa itself where the headquarters of the 313th Air Division was located. Bases were like cities; Kadena Air Base and Naha Air Base, both on Okinawa, were huge.

After being on Okino for a while, I got to know many local people, including a few teachers. In time, I was able to arrange for some of them to visit with the officers on the base for parties. Being assigned to Japan, southern Japan especially, was a cultural shock for me. I saw women doing heavy construction work such as pouring concrete, driving large trucks and other jobs that I saw only men do back in the U.S.A. At the base, most of the service jobs, like working in the kitchen, food preparation, cleaning services and laundry were done by local Japanese people. Most of the American contractors had Japanese women who they maintained off the base.

I spent most of my time when off duty exercising, mostly long-distance running on the road to town and back, a run of approximately eight miles. My runs were done on hilly terrain through farmland. At places, rice was grown and pineapples were a common agricultural product. One day on one of my runs, as I was passing a geisha house, one of its residents came out and solicited me to come in for another type of exercise. She indicated that she had a condom. I turned down the offer and went on with my workout. As I remember, no other officer joined me on any of these runs. I was the only one who exercised like that among the officers on a daily basis. After a year of working out, I was in great physical shape.

The mission of the radar base was defense against an enemy air attack that never came. The only fatality at the base that year was a sergeant by the name of Mulkhurn who committed suicide with poison for reasons that were never disclosed. This remote and tiny base had no library and there was little available to read. However, I got to go to Okinawa at times and thus was able to have a break from Okinoerabujima. On one of my leaves, I even got to go to Hong Kong, which was under British control at the time (1957). I had beautiful clothes made for Joyce and myself, and along with other items, bought Rolex watches for both of us.

When I arrived in Hong Kong, I remember being accosted by prostitutes looking for business. On my return from leave, I continued my normal routine on the base. As with all lieutenants, the base commander had assigned me additional duties, including food service officer and motor pool officer. These were areas where I had no knowledge at all, however, I had sergeants (E-5s) for both of these areas who ran things and took good care. All I ever had to do was sign the papers for those departments.

One night, an enlisted man, a sergeant who was an indigenous person, i.e., a Native American Indian, got drunk and caused a lit cigarette to burn a mattress in the enlisted quarters. Smoking in bed is a courts-martial offense, nevertheless, I did not file charges against him. I just made him pay for the mattress. Even so, he did not appreciate the serious charges that I saved him from. He told me that there were extra mattresses in the supply account. At that time, I was supply officer for the base and could have just let it slide, but I didn't. I made him pay for it. He's lucky I was there because that saved him from more serious legal charges.

One night in the lounge area of the officers' quarters, everyone was having drinks. I was with a group of officers and the commander, who was talking about his experiences in the South Pacific during the Second World War. He said that the native islanders were so repulsive that even the black American soldiers would not fraternize with them. He showed no understanding of people who have been impacted by warfare and have suffered trauma, and he let loose his feelings of low judgment that he had for black soldiers.

࿐࿐࿐

In January of 1958, I was finished with my one-year tour of duty in Japan and was assigned to a base in Texarkana, Arkansas. My arrival in Texarkana was a complete shock for the major in command of the station, and a discomfort to the other officers. They did not expect a black officer to be assigned to this small base of about 150 people. My assignment there was a massive social and cultural upheaval for all the white people at the base, including the local white civilians who worked there.

I arrived on a Saturday afternoon when the commander was not on base. Had I arrived during the week, when the commander was present, this story would have been different. He could have stopped me from signing in and I would have immediately been sent to another base. However, once I signed in, he was stuck with me until the new fiscal year.

First of all, the social life for the officers centered around the local white-only country club. I was not allowed to go to the country club or to be in any social setting with the officers' wives. Here I was in uniform, ready to fight and die for my country at a moment's notice, but for some reason they thought I was a threat to the safety of their wives and children. The only "social event" I was ever invited to on the base was the showing of pornographic films, which I attended once.

The second reason was that they did not want a black man to be in charge of any department that involved the supervision of white civilian employees. The dilemma created by white supremacy was handled by assigning me to a single military duty where I interacted with military personnel only, while other officers had a number of additional duties that included supervising civilian employees. I had less work to prevent me from being the boss of white people; this was the commander's solution to that particular white supremacist dilemma.

White supremacy helped me by making my workload lighter, but it hurt white officers because they had to pick up the slack, *i.e.*, the extra duties that I would have been assigned if everything were done on an equal basis. It was sad to see that many times some white people would disadvantage themselves to maintain segrega-

David D. Strachan

Dizzy Gillespie performing in Atlanta, 1956. This photo was taken by David D. Strachan while stationed in Bainbridge, GA.

Lieutenant Strachan on leave in Hong Kong, September 1957

tionist protocol. At the base where I had been stationed in Georgia, the men's room had a sign that read, "For Colored Only" on the door. I used that men's room, not because I was told to, but because it was absolutely clean, while the other one that was for whites only was subject to heavy traffic due to the fact that there were hundreds of white officers and only one black officer, me.

So, I ended up with a lot less work to do, having just one military duty. The town of Texarkana did not offer much to me in terms of having access to a swimming pool or gymnasium where I could exercise. When off duty, I spent a lot of my time reading in the small base library, which was co-housed in a building with the Base Exchange (BX), that is to say, the military department store. I never set foot in the BX because I had no need to; there was nothing there that I wanted to buy.

I would visit the library on a regular basis to read when off duty. One morning, I was told to report to the orderly room – the commander's office – to see the adjutant. He asked me if I would be willing to answer some questions. I told him to ask his questions. The next thing he said was, "You have the right to remain silent; anything you say can be used against you." I told him at that point to ask his questions. The questions dealt with some thefts that had taken place at the BX. The adjutant was also a first lieutenant, like me.

He went on to inquire about me being in the building on a certain day and whether or not the door to the exchange was open or closed. I told him the door had been open, that I was in the building to read and did see the door to the exchange in the open position. On the day in question, I remembered that a European American, an enlisted man of a low rank, came into the building. While I sat in the room reading, as I usually did, he must have gone to report me as a thief, even though the only crime he saw was me in the act of reading. No one ever talked to me before they read me my rights in preparation for charging me, a first lieutenant, for a crime on the say-so of an enlisted person. Nothing came of the charges. I was transferred to Lackland AFB in San Antonio, Texas, for a second tour there. I believe that the white people at the Arkansas base were glad to see me go. No one said good-bye. The experience taught me that white supremacy was always at work and that, by whatever means they could, they would find a way to get rid of me so that they would again have an all-white officer corps at that particular Air Force base.

കൈകൈ

While I was assigned to Japan, from January 1957 to January 1958, my wife Joyce enrolled at Meharry Medical College in Nashville, Tennessee. At that time, very few women were allowed to enroll in medical school. In a class of about one hundred students, mostly black men, there were maybe three women. The college provided housing for all the male students in a brand new dormitory, but none at all for the female students. Joyce had a difficult time finding somewhere to live. She suffered harassment from her mostly black male classmates. Meharry Medical College at the time was one of two colleges in the U.S.A. that trained black physicians and dentists during this era of racial segregation. Some of her fellow students, I was told, would say things like, "You are taking a man's job by going to medical school." Her life in the fall of 1957 was one of misery because of the lack of support from Meharry, even in helping her look for a place to live. She spent her first semester in medical school sleeping on the couch in someone else's apartment. It was not until January of 1958 that she was able to find a room of her own in the home of Mrs. Menzies, a senior black woman who lived in a house near the campus.

During Christmas-New Year's vacation of 1957-58, Joyce decided to remain in Nashville rather than return to New York City. She was invited to a party by one of the female students in the dental hygienist program at the school. The acceptance of this invitation proved to be one of the greatest mistakes of her life. She told me that the party started at a local restaurant and bar and then moved on to a nearby apartment. Joyce said that she went with the group and did not wake up until late afternoon of the next day. She had her clothes on, but they were in somewhat disarray. She said that her vagina felt irritated. She decided to go to a local doctor and he determined that Joyce had been raped. Joyce was a very trusting, gentle, kind, beautiful person who had been drugged and raped by a man or men while unconscious. She took no action against anyone for this crime and it was not reported to the police.

The young woman, the dental hygiene student who invited her to the party, might have been an accessory by deliberately putting Joyce in harm's way. Perhaps she was serving as a "Judas goat" in the plan to drug and rape Joyce so that she herself would not become the victim. That party was attended by local people Joyce did not know. Local men must have noticed her, a beautiful woman and an outsider in this small community, when she came to Nashville in the fall of 1957. There is little sympathy in white supremacist, apartheid-America, for black women who are sexually attacked at a party. I might also add that DNA-testing was not available in 1957-58.

Joyce never recovered from the rape. The person I knew, loved and married figuratively died after this tragic incident and was never seen again. She carried the wounds of her attack until the day of her death, 9 January 2013. Joyce became a depressed person and often let herself be exploited in dealing with other people in business matters. She became a person who was easy to cheat and steal from. Her eyes looked dead and she often talked to herself. The beautiful, kind, joyful person who would stop traffic on the street was gone. It took Joyce seven years to finish medical school, including an internship, and the stress of being with an injured person took a heavy toll upon me as well as my wounded wife.

In 1960, Joyce gave birth to our first child, Davia. We were very fortunate in receiving great help from Mrs. Menzies until we returned to New York in 1964.

# David D. Strachan

Joyce S. Henry (Strachan), c.1955. The inscription in the upper left reads, "To David, Love Joyce."

1LT David D. Strachan, U.S. Air Force, 313th Air Divison, HQ, Okinawa, Japan, 1957

❧❧❧

I got out of the service in May of 1959 and joined Joyce in Nashville. Nashville, Tennessee in 1959 was as racially segregated as any town in South Africa under apartheid. In the 1960s, the Civil Rights Movement was engaged in attempts to desegregate American institutions in many places, including Nashville. I was present in downtown Nashville one day when a group of young black people who were in the vanguard of this movement, attempting to desegregate a lunch counter, were attacked by a large group of white thugs who were pelting them with rocks as the police at the scene stood by. The next thing I noticed was the police moving in and arresting the black students who were demonstrating, rather than the group of white male thugs who had attacked them. This vision of injustice in the form of white-supremacy racism was driven into my mind and has helped mold me into the fighter for justice that I am.

I was able to get a job at the Wharton Public School in Nashville, where I taught health and physical education. I enjoyed working everyday in this first through ninth grade school. This was a new, but shoddy, public school built for black children in the racially segregated system of schools that characterized the South. The Wharton School at times would receive the old, ragged textbooks that had been discarded by the schools where white children were in attendance.

I was paid about $3,000 a year and it was considered to be a good job for a black man. I was interviewed for the job by the superintendent of schools, an older white man, but the only thing he asked me was what church I belonged to. I told him that I had just gotten out of the military and had not yet selected a church. He seemed satisfied with that answer and gave me the job, which came with no benefits at that time.

For me, it was a feeling of joy to teach as I empowered stu-

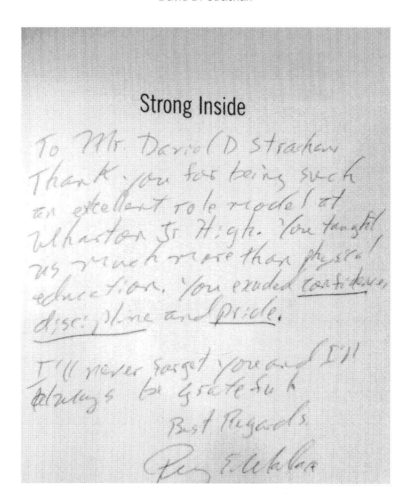

A middle school student in Nashville in 1959, Perry Wallace became the topic of a book by Andrew Maraniss, *Strong Inside: Perry Wallace and the Collision of Race and Sports in the South* (Vanderbuilt University Press, 2014). His inscription inside the book reads, "To Mr. David D. Strachan, Thank you for being such an excellent role model at Wharton Jr. High. You taught us much more than physical education. You exuded confidence, discipline and pride. I'll never forget you and I'll always be grateful. Best Regards, Perry E. Wallace." Professor Wallace teaches at the American University School of Law.

dents to grow and learn new things. For example, I introduced the sport of soccer to black youngsters who had never played it before; many of them had never heard of soccer in 1959. The work I did motivated me to work beyond the school day much of the week, so I took a part-time job in the city-funded recreation center at the school for the sum of $1.10 an hour. That was a wage somewhat lower than what white employees earned, I later found out after seeing some misdirected checks.

Nashville, like so many places in America where white supremacy reigns, at one time openly paid black teachers less than white teachers. The case of the black teachers was taken to court in a suit and the city was told that it had to change its practice. People have a way, however, of going around court orders. Salaries are quite often negotiated under the table and behind closed doors, away from the eyes and ears of public scrutiny.

During the late 1950s and early 60s while I was teaching at Wharton, city government officials did not seem to be very pleased about the prospect of black children using the public swimming pools. As a result of the possibility of black children swimming in the same pools with white children, the city closed the public swimming pools. They built a small outdoor pool a little bigger than a large bathtub at the Wharton School for the black children. As I remember events, it seems to me that most of the children who drowned that summer, because they swam in unsafe places like rivers and streams, were not the black children.

∽∾∽∾

In the summer of 1963, I came back to New York to earn some money, which I needed. Teachers in Nashville, as I mentioned, had zero benefits and were not paid for the months of July and August. One of the jobs I did in New York was to drive a great big, yellow Checker taxicab. You can learn a lot about the people you pick up while driving a cab. For example, the most generous people are working-class people, while the richest people are the cheapest and they will fight you to get a nickel change. I tried to avoid drunks, who may throw up in your cab, in *my* cab.

On 28 August 1963, I returned to Nashville by way of the March on Washington. I was able to get up close to the front of the event and see Dr. Martin Luther King, Jr. give his famous *I Have a Dream* speech. When I got back to Nashville, some of my co-workers told me they had seen me on television while watching the event.

Students from Wingate High School prepare for a lesson with their flight instructor in the late 1990s at Republic Airport, Farmingdale, New York.

# Chapter Two:
## *Look Who They Sent Us Now*

Before I left active duty with the Air Force in 1959, I joined the Aeroclub at Lackland Air Force Base in San Antonio and paid the cost of earning my Federal Aviation Administration (FAA) certification for single-engine airplane, that is to say, a private pilot's license. In July 1964, Joyce finished her internship as a physician at Hubbard Hospital in Nashville and the three of us, my daughter Davia, Joyce and I, went back to New York and lived with Joyce's mother in Haverstraw, New York. I enrolled at Columbia University Teachers' College and got a Master of Arts degree in administration. Joyce became a resident physician in psychiatry at Rockland State Hospital in Rockland County.

I soon took a position as a teacher in the Industrial Arts department of a local school district and worked there for two years. Then I went to a number of FAA private schools to earn numerous certificates with my own funds. Only a small portion of my aeronautical training was paid for by the G.I. Bill, which kicked in only after I had already begun my training.

I earned FAA certificates in many areas. I first became a private pilot, sea and land airplane. I became a helicopter pilot. I became a commercial pilot single-engine and multi-engine, sea and land. I also got my instrument rating. In addition to that, I went to agricultural pilot school and graduated as an agricultural pilot. I also earned instructor ratings in three areas: airplane instructor for single-engine, land and sea; instrument instructor; and lastly, multi-engine instructor. All of these are separate licenses. I took written, practical and oral examinations for all three of these instructor ratings. I proved to myself that the Air Force was wrong in what they had said about me and in expelling me from the pilot-training program in Georgia, where I had been subject to racist abuse.

About that time, Joyce got a job at the State Hospital in the Bronx and we moved from Rockland County and went to live in the Bronx. I took a position in 1967 as a teacher in a junior high school in the area of health and physical education. I left that position and moved on to a teaching position in the attendance bureau of the Board of Education in the South Bronx. Most of my time there was spent investigating children who were not attending school, and doing what I could to assist them. Each day I got to assist poor people with all the social and economic problems they suffered. It did not take me long to understand that poor people live under a system that is designed to keep them poor or nearly poor. It is an oppressive system and I would see it everyday when I worked among them. Poor peoples' children, as a rule, do not do as well in school as those children who do not have the massive problems related to a lack of money, as well as those of a social nature. In today's world, the current practice is for those who rule America to scapegoat teachers and never analyze the real reasons why poor students do not perform well.

As a bureaucrat, I was shuffling papers and not actually solving the real problems of my clients. Sometime around 1970, I took a position as a teacher in a drug program at Evander Childs High School in the Bronx, the SPARK program, and I became the lead facilitator in that program for the Board of Education. It gave me an opportunity to help many young people by opening doors to numerous positive activities for them. This involved career counseling, frequent field trips, travel and doing things that were uplifting and beneficial to the students.

This was a great program. It involved all kinds of activities, including taking students to Broadway shows. We would go to senior citizen residences and meet with senior citizens. We had much group counseling and my day had no limit on the number of hours that I worked because I enjoyed what I was doing so much. Also,

Joyce Strachan in the Bronx, c.1970

"Mom," Joyce, c.1968. Photo courtesy of David D. Strachan, Jr.

Mr. and Mrs. David D. Strachan and family in the Bronx, c.1970. Twins David D. Strachan, Jr. and Dina sit on their father's and mother's laps, respectively; elder sister Davia is to the right.

I introduced some of them to the possibility of becoming pilots, either as a career or for recreation. I took many of them flying for a free introductory lesson. No funding was provided for this activity, so I paid for it out of my own pocket.

In 1975, the New York City Board of Education experienced a huge budget crisis, leading to the laying off of many teachers and other personnel, and my program was cut back to bare bones. At that point, I was forced to leave. I found a position as a mathematics teacher in a small Brooklyn school located in Bushwick. After working for about a year in the mathematics department, I was transferred to Boys and Girls High School in Bedford-Stuyvesant, Brooklyn, where I was assigned to the social studies department. There I started a course in aviation technology. The course gave students a chance to have free flight lessons given by me. The cost of renting the aircraft was paid for by the students selling candy bars. This worked out well, with the exception of one student who did not return the money for the candy he sold.

During my second year at Boys and Girls High, a new principal was assigned to the school and the aviation program was eliminated. The new principal was not interested in introductory aviation classes, so I spent the school year as a social studies teacher. In June, I got a call from the assistant principal at Wingate High School, also in Brooklyn, about a job as a teacher of flight technology. I accepted the offer and was overjoyed with the chance to train young people. Later on, I found out that I was replacing a white airline pilot who had been laid off from his commercial job and had to leave the teaching job because he had been called back.

I felt this was the best job I had ever been offered. It helped to heal the grief and pain I was still feeling from the daggers of racism that had nearly killed me in the U.S. Air Force. I felt it was a chance for relief from the negative things that had happened to me. This job I saw as a chance to redeem myself and turn the tables on the racists who had tried to destroy me. However, my main mission was to empower the young people in this nearly one hundred per cent black and Latino school and to train them to negotiate the minefield ahead of them, if they wanted to have an aviation career in a white-dominated society like this one. Most of them did not have a clue about how racism works or what one has to do to succeed in getting around it. I believed then and I still believe now that learning these life skills was just as important as learning flight technology. Many black children in America are not taught the necessity of dealing with white-supremacy racism and have to learn the hard way.

As a way to empower my students, I felt it was important for them to learn how white-supremacy racism has played out in aviation history, including up to the present day. I taught them the Ashanti proverb I had learned to drive home my point: *When the fool learns the game, the players have dispersed*. I made them write it down.

The first day of class was my introduction, I felt, to seeing many damaged black teenagers who were suffering from the internalized oppression and/or self-hatred that was caused by the underside of racism. I learned that some students did not like the idea that I was replacing the white teacher they had had in the previous term. In a loud whisper, I overheard one of them say, "Look who they sent us now." Some of them felt they were being short-changed by getting a black teacher. I was asked many times if I was even a pilot, and it took me some time to prove to those students that I actually was. Finally, I decided to bring in my FAA aeronautical certificates, *i.e.*, my licenses, to show to the students.

I threw myself into my teaching far beyond the normal workday. There was a flight-training device, a simulator, in my classroom and I used it to teach instrument flying to small groups during class. I found that my students were brilliant. They learned quickly and performed like skilled instrument pilots. I was overjoyed with the performance of many of them.

I had a passion for teaching. I enjoyed teaching flight technology so much that if I could have done it without getting paid for it, I would have, but I needed the money. Some teachers at this segre-

Flight instructors and their students at Moton Field during the fly-in conducted by the Negro Airmen's International (NAI) in Tuskegee, Alabama. The diminutive woman in the center is Melva Hill Jackman, former president of the New York chapter of NAI. Directly behind her is Enrique Ballenilla and to his left is Franklin Rodriguez.

Left: Wingate pilot Anthony Robinson (l.) takes a break with the legendary "Chief" Anderson at Moton Field in Tuskegee, Alabama. Right: Franklin Rodriguez (l.) confers with David D. Strachan during the fly-in over Moton Field. Many of David's students built up their hours by working as flight instructors, either at Moton Field or at AATC.

gated high school were sad every day they came to work. Many of them expressed a sense of disbelief when I shared with them my passion for those students who wanted to be pilots. Some would make a joke out of my goal of empowering students to fulfill their desire for an aviation career. One of my colleagues, when he saw what I was doing with the simulator, exclaimed, "Oh, that's too hard for them to learn." Another teacher made the comment that advanced mathematics is best taught in the suburbs, not in schools in the "inner city," which is code for where black people live. One administrator suggested I teach my students how to march.

There were teachers, counselors and administrators, nevertheless, who were very supportive of my mission to empower and motivate students and assist those who wanted to be aviators. Mr. Glen Goldberg was one, as were Miss Flo Waxman and Miss Hazel Chambers. My classroom was one where I referred to students as scholars. I spent a great deal of time empowering them by teaching them how to negotiate the minefield of white-supremacy racism that they live with here in the U.S.A., especially in the field of aviation, but everywhere. I taught them the history of aviation and the role of black people in that history.

My discussions with students included the long history of employment discrimination against black people in the field of aviation, discrimination that goes on to this day. Lessons included discussions about the Tuskegee Airmen; about Bessie Coleman, the famous black woman pilot; about Chief Albert Anderson of Tuskegee Institute, who taught himself to fly; and about Marlon Green, one of the first black commercial airline pilots in America, who had to sue the airlines to force them to hire him. I taught them about many other black aviators and I made them understand that black aviators today stand upon the shoulders of those who have gone before. For some of them, it was very difficult to get the message across when I talked about the practice of white supremacy in the field of aviation. I had to make them understand that you have to know the game and know how to go around, go under, or go through the barriers. I drove home the message that no one was ever going to make it easy for them.

Some students would say that I was prejudiced against white people and a racist when I covered subjects that touched upon race. One student went to an administrator to complain and told him that he did not want to learn anything about black pilots; he was interested in learning about white pilots only. Needless to say, this was a black student. I was called into the administrator's office regarding this complaint. In response, I said just one thing: "I believe that this student is suffering from internalized oppression." I made the administrator understand that what he was seeing was self-hatred and hatred of others, me for example, who looked like him. That was the end of the complaint against me.

Everyday, I would drive home the point that was taught to me by the great minister, Rev. Dr. Eric Butterworth, one of the mentors of Maya Angelou: *You can do anything that anyone else has done.* I'd drive that lesson into them every single day. A day never went by that I failed to motivate my students.

I had an uphill battle, not only against the damage done to my students by racism, economic deprivation and social problems, but also the negative effects of some parents. For example, some of my students were being told that being a pilot was not an attainable goal for black boys. One of them, as I remember, came to me and said in a whining voice, "Mommy says that being a pilot is for white boys." That's hard to go up against. One student was told by her parents, in my presence, that being a pilot was not for girls. I interrupted and told them that there were many female pilots who could fly all types of aircraft, from the Piper Cub to the Boeing 747. Some had become bomber pilots and fighter pilots. I told them that women had the ability to achieve a pilot career just as men did, and I told her that she should not let anyone tell her what she couldn't do. I made a special effort to encourage the small number of females in my classes. It was not easy to get the message over to girls that they could do just as well as boys in learning to be a pilot. One girl, Diane, told me that her father had decided that she should be a nurse. She defied him and took my recommendation to attend Alabama Aviation and Technical College (AATC). That was a good choice for pilot training at that time because of its low tuition and fees.

I helped all of my students – those who listened – make selections for appropriate pilot training schools at low-cost state institutions. Very few got caught going to an expensive, private college when they could get the same education, and their pilot's licenses, for less money. Those students who listened, the ones who did not get caught in the minefield that I warned them about beforehand and fall by the wayside, accomplished the goal of becoming a pilot. I drummed into the heads of all my students that to achieve this goal, you must keep your eye on the goal and not get caught up with social issues like how many country girls you can take to bed. I warned them, "School before girls." Many of my students graduated with all the aeronautical credentials (licenses) they needed to start a career. Some of them went on to get their baccalaureate and master's degrees after finishing their associate's degree at AATC as professional pilots.

During the time my students were at college, they kept in touch with me by telephone. I was told by some of them that the majority of black students in pilot training at the college were my students, not at the college in general, but in the pilot training department. I believe that the staff at AATC saw this as something that was unusual down in Alabama, that is to say, more black students than white students in the pilot-training section of the school. Soon I was receiving invitations to AATC to lecture and hold workshops for its students. I was also asked to speak at various local schools and given the Key to the City of Ozark, Alabama. One year, I was invited to be the commencement speaker at the college's graduation. The graduates at that ceremony were mostly white youngsters and they and their guests had their eyes riveted upon me during my entire address. I gave a speech related to doing whatever it takes

Wingate pilot Diane Pencil visits David D. Strachan at his home,
September 2008.

David D. Strachan visits one of his former students, Ewan Duncan,
inside a Federal Correctional Institute, April 2007.

to reach one's positive goals in life. I spoke with a cadence and words that got everyone's attention. Every eye was glued upon me. I've done enough public speaking to know when people are paying attention, and this was one of those moments when I had them "locked in" on what I was saying.

Later on, I served as a volunteer counselor for AATC at numerous college fairs held in high schools throughout New York City. My experience in attending college fairs was that students were mostly impressed by the size of the displays brought by other colleges to the fair. Many of the colleges were trying to recruit students for their schools, despite huge tuitions that would lead the students down the path of lifetime debt for something they could obtain less expensively at state colleges or city colleges. Many students at these fairs ignored what I wanted to show them about having an aviation career.

After graduation from AATC, many of my former students began to get jobs as flight instructors as a stepping-stone to the end goal of being an airline pilot. It was a happy day for both of us when my first student got a job at a small regional airline. As time went on, those who cracked open the door reached back and helped others get past this barrier that was, and still is, in place for black pilots and women pilots. Racism was so strong in the mid-part of the 20th century, after the Second World War, that airlines would train white males with zero flying experience rather than hire a skilled and experienced black pilot such as Marlon Green or one of the Tuskegee Airmen, who were available and qualified. It was not easy.

Many of my students tried numerous times before getting a pilot's job, but as time moved on, the door opened up, a little, in the airline industry as well as the military. I taught them the game as teenagers and they played it well. Persistence had been drilled into their heads. I still keep contact with many of them. I feel like a father bird that has taught his chicks to fly.

It gives me a sense of pleasure to know that I was able to

David D. Strachan (r.) gets a visit from Wingate
pilot, Anthony Hunter.

David D. Strachan (l.) attends the wedding of a Wingate pilot with the late Leroy
Kinlocke, one of the first to graduate from Wingate High School and attend
AATC. O'Neil Barnes describes Leroy as "the glue" that held the Wingate
students together in Alabama. Leroy's untimely death in New Zealand in 2012
left a hole in the David D. Strachan legacy.

out-maneuver our enemy in America's system of white supremacy. In my passion for teaching young people to reach their goals, some students who were planning to apply for a pilot job would come to my home and I would help them prepare a laser-like résumé no longer than one page. I was good at résumé-writing for my students. Many got the job. Today, many of my students fly all kinds of aircraft, including the Boeing 747 and the Airbus 320. These students grew up in segregated neighborhoods which some people call "the ghetto," with all of its social and economic implications. These students were told that they were "not good enough" to be pilots. This out-maneuvering was payback for the same thing that I was told about myself, payback for what was done to me in Georgia in 1956 when I was sent to pilot training there. My experience at Bainbridge AFB has turned into a victory for me because the racist instructors at Bainbridge thought they'd destroyed me and gotten rid of one black person. I survived and thrived. Now the airline industry has to deal with hundreds of black pilots as a result of the program I ran at Wingate H.S. In addition, over the years I've counseled young men and women who were not my students at Wingate, giving them valuable information that has played an important role in their lives and been a key factor in putting them on the right track to a pilot's career.

I've been called on the telephone from many places, including foreign countries, and people I've never met would ask me for information about pilot training. By chance, I've met students at the airport who were enrolled in programs at colleges that were very expensive and/or did not meet their needs in reaching the goal of becoming a pilot. I've "stolen" students from schools that were bad choices they had made or were referred to by "misguidance" counselors, professional educators who were completely blind when it came to counseling students about pilot training. Also, many parents would give advice about aviation careers even though they knew nothing about it. At one time I was a very active member of the Negro Airmen's International (NAI) and in that capacity, I

Education never ceases. Above: David D. Strachan visits AATC after retirement to conduct a workshop. Several of his former students from Wingate High School attended the session. Below: His student, Diane Pencil, center, returns to Brooklyn in captain's uniform to inspire adult students at the College of New Rochelle's School of Continuing Resources Brooklyn Campus, March 2015. David D. Strachan is in the back row, second from right.

would guide many people through their aviation career plans.

My passion for helping and guiding others grew ever stronger each day with the indelible memory of the brush-off I got from the only black pilot I had known at NYU. Lack of good advice can be fatal for a person seeking a pilot's career. I felt like I was rising from the ashes as I counseled people about pilot training. It is important to note that those who belong to the same demographic group as you may not care or be able to help you. Some good people can be found in every demographic group, so you can't go by the color of someone's skin in making judgments. There are good people to be found everywhere, including in aviation.

My mission as a teacher and counselor has been consistent with the goal of empowering students and others that I touch. Empowering people brings great joy to my life. I have helped many people of all colors. Many of these people have had financial challenges, but that has not always been the case. One day, a young white man was referred to me for counseling. I told him about a pilot training program that would be good for him to enroll in. He asked me how much it would cost. I gave him an estimate of the cost and he said, "Fine." The next thing I knew, he was out the door on his way to his grandmother's house to get a check for the full amount needed for the program I had recommended. I can't remember any of my black students being so fortunate as to have a grandmother wealthy enough to write a check for the full cost of their education.

In my classroom, the main parts of the curriculum were divided into compartments. The three main compartments were motivation, technology and drill on flight maneuvers. My teaching was redundant. Everyone got to go to Republic Airport in Farmingdale, Long Island at least once for a flying lesson. It was drilled into every student's head that when he or she was selected to go to the airport with the class, they were not going for a joyride; they were going to learn how to be a pilot. In order for students to continue getting these free flying lessons, they had to first recite the various flight maneuvers and how to do them. They were expected to learn the names of the maneuvers and how to do them before getting into the cockpit of the airplane. If they did well in the classroom, it was a ticket to additional flying lessons. All the lessons were free of charge to the students, nevertheless, due to social or economic factors in the lives of many of them, some would not take advantage of the expensive lessons that were paid for by the Board of Education.

My program was like unlocking a door to opportunity and swinging it open for all to enter, however, not everyone could take advantage of this golden opportunity. Some students would fail to show up when scheduled to go on the free school bus to the airport. Needless to say, a student who was a no-show without a good reason had little chance of being rescheduled. I found out early in the program that a significant number of students would be late for the 6:00 a.m. appointment I set for them to pick up the headset that I provided for them, free of charge, before we were ready to depart for the airport. I made a policy that the bus left at 7:00 a.m. sharp and did not wait for latecomers. At 7:00 a.m., when the school bus started moving, it did not stop, even if you were fifty yards away and running to catch the bus. This was my way of drilling the idea of punctuality into the heads of my students. Every flight student got the message that pilots have to be on time for their scheduled flights.

As soon as the bus moved from in front of the school building on its trip to the airport, I always talked to the students about flight maneuvers. I would get them fired up about becoming pilots. I never just sat there on the ride to Republic Airport without coaching them. At the airport, some Long Island schools brought mostly all-white classes of students to the contractors where they were receiving some type of service, not always pilot training. I never saw any group as well behaved and professionally dressed as my students. I required my students to wear shoes, not sneakers, black pants, and white shirts with ties, even the girls.

Some flight instructors did not appear very interested in teaching my students. They were more interested in taking a long cross-country flight to use up the time, rather than working on maneuvers. Some were caught by my students putting down more time for a lesson than they had actually flown. I trained my students to read the Hobbs meter in the airplane to be able to determine the length of time the lesson had lasted. They were instructed to make sure it matched what the instructor wrote down in their logbooks, which were provided for them. At this particular school, the contractor did not solo students. All of my students had the necessary FAA medical certification required for soloing. I was very disappointed with this contractor who would not solo my students. This contractor also did not hire black instructors. After I complained about the lack of diversity in the instructional staff, they finally hired one black instructor.

After a number of years of using the same contractor in Farmingdale, I felt it was time to move on to a new flight-training contractor at the same airport. The contractor selected was called Flight Ways, a commercial firm that offered many services in the area of aviation business, including soloing students. I knew before I got there that they also refused to hire black flight instructors. I knew this because a number of my students who had graduated from college with all their instructor credentials, and were well qualified, were turned away from instructor positions at Flight Ways.

Once the new contract was put into effect, I took care of this problem of racial discrimination by often standing in flight operations and talking *really* loudly to management about the lack of diversity among the flight instructor staff at this company that had a government contract that called for no racial discrimination. They could not shut me up from talking loudly about this concern of mine in front of their commercial customers. It did not take long before they hired more and more black instructors and other people of color. After a year, at least half the instructors were nonwhite. A black instructor was appointed as chief instructor, even. I believe that most of the instructors of color who were hired do not know how the door to the flight-instructor job was opened up for them. It does not dawn upon people to understand that someone else had to part the way. Some people of color think it was only because they were good, smart or qualified.

After the diversity issue was resolved, the contractor made improvements for my students. Many were able to solo and we had a full complement of great instructors, white and black. I felt good about this latest victory, however small, over white-supremacy racism.

Many students soloed. One young woman was featured in a Board of Education film that was aired on television. The *Daily News* did an article with a picture of one of my students in an airplane with one of the new black instructors who had been hired after I enlightened the contractor. I felt like I was "on a roll" with my students learning to be pilots and doing well. Many were passing their FAA written examinations that I administered free of charge to all of them. (I was an FAA-designated examiner for the written exams at the time.) It was a joy for me to see how the training I had given these young people from Brooklyn empowered them in reaching their professional goals.

While supervising flight operations for my students at Republic Airport, there were few who did not solo. I was led to believe that their performance was not up to standards for solo flight. On further investigation, however, I found that three instructors did not solo any of the contract students. It took me a while to figure out that there was nothing wrong with my students; it was this small group of instructors who did not want to do the work required to train these youngsters to solo. I found this out after the training was over, and I'm sorry that I was not able to intervene in their training and terminate those instructors when I had the chance.

The students who graduated from Wingate during my tenure there went on to college and were successful in completing their aviation training, most of them at Alabama Aviation and Technical College, but a few of them in Oklahoma or other southern states. As time moved on, many of my students began to get jobs as pilots, doing various things like flying bank checks at night and flying charters for companies and small airlines. Many continued to help each other by walking applications for pilot jobs into the human resources department where they were already working. It was not easy; you just had to be persistent to get a job as a pilot.

If you got a pilot job, being a black person, you were always under a microscope: They were always trying to find a reason to fire you. This caused some black pilots to feel that they had to be better than white pilots. If you were black, you had to be a quick learner. There are some people out in the world who do what they can to sabotage you at all levels, including not sharing information with you that you need to do your job. Some racists cannot stand you being there as a pilot at flight operations. It does not feel right to them under the system of white-supremacy racism that is still in effect. For many white people, black people are supposed to have the leftover jobs after the white people have taken what they want. One of my students told me that a white pilot who was enraged at the airline company where they both worked said to him that black people were taking his job.

Another one of my students who is a captain flying a jumbo jet told me a story of how white-supremacist racism follows you even to the level of captain. This is what happened: We know that pilots have to go to the training center once a year for a refresher course on the aircraft they fly. He was assigned to a racist instructor for training. During the training, he noticed this instructor was super-critical of him and he complained to the head instructor about this. Before my student was reassigned to another instructor, the racist instructor told another white pilot who happened to be taking the same refresher course that he planned to get rid of my student during the training. He did not know that the white pilot was married to a black woman and was what we call an "ally" of black people. The racist instructor told the white pilot exactly what he had in mind to do and the white pilot was able to warn my student. So it never ends. No matter where you are in rank, white-supremacy racism is always operating.

Anthony Manswell was the first student of mine to finish Air Force pilot training. It was a triumph for me to attend his graduation in Texas. Before he left for training, I briefed him well. I told him months ahead of time that I wanted him to send for all the manuals and books that were being used at the Air Force pilot training base he was going to. He was instructed by me to study all these materials before reporting for training. This is part of my practice in counseling all my students, to be ahead of the game. Today, Anthony is captain of a jumbo jet and flies all over the world.

It is wonderful to know that many of my students are flying *over* Riker's Island, rather than being in it. For those who don't know what Riker's Island is, it is a jail located near LaGuardia Airport in Queens, New York.

During the many years I was a teacher, I was very joyful about serving my students and I always believed that they could accomplish their goals. I have a love for my students that is like the love I have for my consanguineous children. I think that one of the secrets of being a good teacher is you have to love the people you are teaching. All my students were given my home telephone number and they or their parents could call me at any time. Many still call me from various places in the world as they captain aircraft. These days, I talk with some of them overseas via Skype®.

I've been told by many people that the names of most of their teachers have been forgotten. I'm happy that I am not on the list of forgotten names. When we get together at reunions, I'm always reminded by my students of the lessons they learned from me in class. In some cases, I do not remember exactly what I taught them at that time, but they have not forgotten. It's always a joy.

During my tenure at Wingate, I went to many meetings where

Wingate High School Reunions. Back row, left to right: Ian Abraham, Anthony Manswell, David D. Strachan, Neal Hagley, Enrique Ballenilla, and Leaford Daley. Front row: All but Richard A. John (second from right) are unidentified.

David D. Strachan and former students. Police Officer Ossie Fletcher (second from right) taught for many years at Boys' and Girls' High School in Brooklyn and later did public relations for District Attorney Charles Hynes.

I was able to talk about the successes of my students. I would always take note of the reaction of the "educators" present at these meetings. More than once, certain people made negative remarks, for example, "Oh, flying is too dangerous," or projected the body language of total indifference. Hearing me talk about helping black children in a poor, segregated neighborhood make that trip from the street corner to the captain's seat of a jumbo jet was difficult for some people to grasp. Some seemed rather shocked to hear about the accomplishments of these students from this school. Many people who teach have low expectations of the students with whom they work. They don't expect to see them succeed, especially not as pilots flying Boeing 747s.

It is not easy to overcome internalized oppression, that is to say, the self-hatred that is ingrained in many black people, children and adults. The process of learning to hate oneself becomes natural, especially in a system where the schools are based on a curriculum that emphasizes Europe and essentially delivers a white-supremacist education. Many times, their own racism has made white people feel a sense of cognitive dissonance when seeing something they think is out of order, such as a black person who holds a great position with a high salary and generous benefits. For whatever reason, these positions, in their minds, should be reserved for white people only.

In the study of American history, true American history, one learns that the foundation of this country involved creating a policy of genocide against the indigenous people and stealing their lands, as well as kidnapping Africans, torturing them into submission, and enslaving them for profit. This behavior was codified beginning in the 17th century and was enforced by policies that divided people, Europeans and Africans in particular. Those codes continue to subjugate people of African descent until this day.

Careful study of U.S. history tells us that the resources of African people, for hundreds of years, have been stolen. This country has never sought justice for African-descendant children or adults. At the airport where I took my students for lessons, or at the school, I cannot remember many encouraging words that would empower my pilot-training students. There were exceptions, like Glen Goldberg, a supervisor who gave one hundred per cent support to my program.

One Tuesday afternoon, I was returning from the airport with some of my students who had taken flight lessons that day. As the bus pulled up, a crew from a major television station was waiting in front of the school, but it was clear that they were not there to record images of well-groomed, disciplined students coming back from an airport where they were learning to fly. They were there because there had been some disturbance at the school that day. The corporate media was interested only in school violence; my students were totally ignored.

During the last decade of the $20^{th}$ century, I was able to expand the program to include new young flight technology teachers, including Guy Bellegrave, Lavere Dean and Brian Leanders. These young teachers were a great asset to the flight technology program at Wingate H.S. In June 1996, I retired from the NYC public school system and it was not long after that that the Board of Education terminated the program at Wingate. This was a loss for students aiming for an aviation career. After I retired, but before the flight program ended, City Council representative Una Clarke helped the program obtain a brand new flight simulator. After the program was terminated, this expensive device fell silent and out of service.

One day, when I was in dialogue with one of my former students who is a pilot with the U.S. Air National Guard and a jumbo jet pilot for a major airline, he asked me an important question: *"Why would the Department of Education terminate a program that had so much success in launching the aviation careers of so many poor black students?"* My response was clear: I told him that we live in a country where those in power are not committed to empowering people they've always exploited, and that certainly also includes the children of those people. The plan is not set up for children of color to reach for the stars. The U.S. spends billions of dollars a year to incarcerate people of color rather than train them to be airline pilots or otherwise self-sufficient. It did not take long after my departure to remove the flight program at Wingate and get back to the usual business of education, that is, running a school-to-prison pipeline for black children.

When I was still teaching in the flight program at Wingate, I was doing much more than teaching just aviation technology. I spent time teaching my students how to write letters to people like the superintendent of the district in support of their flight-training program. At times, I would have them write two or three drafts before I provided a stamped envelope for their finished product. I kept a deluge of letters going to the Board of Education office in the district. These things were not in the curriculum, however, they helped keep the program alive each year I was there. Once I was no longer there, the program was on track to death row and finally, it was terminated, but not before I was able to graduate hundreds of black boys and girls and watch many of them rise successfully from the neighborhood to the cockpit.

Many parents of my students were very supportive of their child's career goals in the field of aviation. Some parents I was able to turn from negative to positive in support of a child's career plans. On one occasion, a student brought his mother to talk to me about him wanting to go to college to study for a professional pilot career. She said, "Mr. Strachan, do think he can do this?" She continued by saying that the family thought the best career path for him was to join the military. I spoke to them for a long time with positive talk about going forward with an aviation education. The next day, he brought her back to my classroom in the afternoon after the last class for another dose of my motivational presentation. I won. His mother eventually dropped the idea of him going into the military after graduation from high school, she supported him in college, and he was the first of my students to get an airline pilot's job. In the latter part of his career, he finished up as captain of a jumbo jet.

Not all of my students' stories had such a happy ending. Living in the Crown Heights section of Brooklyn is tantamount to living in one of New York City's internal colonies, *i.e.*, ghettos, designated for black people and often leading to tragedy and violence. A student by the name of Sheldon was one of the Wingate scholars due to graduate and go on to Alabama Aviation and Technical College (AATC), where he had been accepted, when he was shot and killed at a party because he did not give up his coat and jewelry quickly enough while being robbed. Wingate lost one of its best pilots through this senseless violence. No one was ever arrested or convicted for Sheldon's murder.

Some of my students went home each day and talked with their parents about the things they were learning in my class. Most parents were concerned and supportive of their youngsters' aviation ambitions without extra meetings with me. The students who listened and kept in contact with me when they arrived at AATC did well and avoided being blown to angry pieces in the racist minefields of the state of Alabama. I received regular phone calls from students who wanted to talk about how things were going while they were away at college. Most of them were able to obtain funds to pay for their flight training by way of loans.

I saw that problems always arose when the student lost sight of his or her goals and became distracted by buying a used car and/or romancing the local country girls. The lesson that was drummed into the heads of my students was to never lose sight of what the goal is. Do not let cars or sex or anger or anything else stop you from graduating. My relationship with most of them was not just that of teacher and counselor to them and their families; I felt like a lifeguard on duty to protect them from the pitfalls. Most of them in high school had been assigned to a so-called "guidance" counselor for academic and career guidance; they did not get to pick and chose the person who was entrusted with giving them information. In many cases, these counselors turned out to be "misguidance" counselors who misled students because they knew nothing about aviation education, and did not know that they didn't know anything. This included not counseling students about the availability of the flight class. Taking advice from the wrong person in high school can destroy a student's entire career, and his or her life.

Some of my students had been misled by sales people who were working for profit-making flight schools. A student can spend huge sums of money gotten from various sources and end up with nothing by going to the wrong school. For example, one of my students who would not listen to me went to an expensive private college for flight training and soon dropped out with nothing to show for it but a big bill. Another young man was referred to me for help after he had borrowed a large sum of money for flight training and paid it to a flight school that went bankrupt with his borrowed money. The lesson here is that those who tried to reinvent the wheel and did not learn the game of flight training in my class were seldom heard from again. I hope they are doing well and do not duck around the corner if they see me while walking down the street.

Many students have been very grateful for the help they received from me. I've been invited many times to visit with them in their palatial homes in various parts of the country. After two or three days of what I think is near-royal treatment, I feel uncomfortable and head back to my own home in New York City. One of my students even ordered a limousine for me on one of my visits, something I never expected, but there it was. On another visit to a different student, he, his wife and his children vacated their bedroom suite and slept in the living room area of his beautiful home so that I would not be disturbed while I slept. Meals at one home I remember very clearly were like a five-star hotel banquet, including anything I wanted to drink. The children of the family were not allowed to sit at the dinner table while I dined.

Each day I celebrate the achievements of my students in the

David D. Strachan, Neal Hagley
and Ian Abraham at Neal's wedding

Neville Giles and his bride with
Mr. Strachan

David D. Strachan regularly attends the nuptial ceremonies of his former
students. Here he poses with (l. to r.) Jason Matthews, Anthony Hunter, Leroy
Kinlocke, Wayne Brown, and Berton Lumsden at Wayne's wedding.

field of aviation. Many have become captains and have also reached back to help others move forward. Other students have decided to go into fields other than aviation and are doing well. They have, in some cases, decided they did not want to be pilots, but wanted to get involved in entrepreneurship, banking, real estate, or other vocations, and that's beautiful and wonderful, but I think they benefited from what they learned in my class. I look forward to a day when students will be able to advance themselves with education paid for by the government, not the system of loans we have that adversely affects everyone. There is no reason why we should have a private education system that is based on making insurance companies and banks rich off the backs of students who want to contribute something to society.

As an aviation educator in Brooklyn, I observed many brilliant students who were unable to pursue a pilot career due to the massive social and economic problems put upon them and their young minds and bodies. Some of them have done well in public and private sector jobs and I celebrate their success there. Others, I find, have done a Herculean job of defeating the social and economic circumstances they were born into, to achieve the goal of becoming a professional pilot. I know students who have faced applying a hundred times before getting a job as a pilot. I salute the persistence they displayed in reaching their goal despite the many obstacles that were placed in their path.

It is important for me to acknowledge that there are many white allies who have been very helpful to these black pilots. One of my former students told me that he was in a group of pilots he worked with at an airline that was going out of business. They went to a start-up airline and were being evaluated for pilot positions at this new airline. After their credentials were reviewed, the company offered jobs to all of the white pilots. The one black pilot, my former student, was not offered a job. One of his white colleagues who had just been hired proved to be an ally and was brave enough to walk back into the human resources office and ask why the one black pilot had not been included in the job offer. This white man showed a tremendous amount of bravery; he could have been fired before he even started! There was a risk of him losing *his* job for what he saw was an injustice being done to another human being, but the human resources department backed down and hired my former student also.

White pilots who are excellent instructors to all student pilots, regardless of the melanin content of their skin, I call mavericks. I salute them. They are valuable allies and I appreciate the help they have given to my students and other black pilots. This is very important to me because I know, living in the U.S.A. where white-supremacy racism is still very much in effect, that there are people, including flight instructors, who don't want to see African Americans achieve success in a field that has *de facto* been reserved for white people. I learned from a white ally one time that he overheard another white flight instructor say that he was not going to teach his black students anything while he worked in the Wingate H.S. program. I believe there have been some instructors who have failed every black student assigned to them, regardless of ability. It is no different from what happens when some police officers specialize in stopping, ticketing, frisking, and arresting black people. As I view it, we live in a country where black people and other people of color are caught in a system that directs many of us to the least satisfying jobs in the service sector. The practice of racism in effect here is fully supported by those who run the country. It is an efficient and wonderful tool that divides the people of America and keeps control in the hands of the plutocrats, to this day, to the detriment of all people regardless of color.

Some of my pilots have told me that, while in the cockpit with white pilots who express an interest in how they were able to get to the captain's seat, it gives them a chance to talk about the training they received at Wingate H.S., including the person (me) who was their teacher and mentor. This is always amazing to some people. Black pilots were the ones who sued the airlines for racial discrimination and won for all discriminated groups, including white women, who stormed the cockpits once the doors were opened to everyone. White women owe gratitude to black men for opening those doors. It is important to understand that white men did not want women to have pilot jobs as well. White women have benefited to the point that their numbers have now surpassed the number of black pilots in the cockpit.

৵৵৵

My experience with racism in the United States Air Force from 1956 to 1959, and especially at Bainbridge Air Base, delivered many wounds to my mind and damage to my body, as well as to my feeling of self-esteem. Unlike many, *many* black men however, I was able to recover. I got much help from various sources including groups like re-evaluation counseling, and by studying the empowering messages of teachers such as Dr. John Henrik Clarke, Dr. Ben Jochannan and Dr. Eric Butterworth. I feel like a wounded lion that has recovered to a condition of being even stronger, and I have become a lifelong warrior in the battle against white supremacy. After being left for dead, I was not only able to revive myself, but also to empower many "cubs," that is, student scholars, to inflict serious damage on the practice of white supremacy with their achievements in the cockpits of commercial airplanes and military aircraft. Those people whose goal it was to destroy me have lost this battle because they now have to deal with hundreds of black pilots, my former students, who would have never succeeded without the benefit of my negative experiences in ROTC and the Air Force. My journey from near defeat to helping others achieve victory has brought joy to my heart. I am pleased that many of my students have learned the game and I can say that it is a great feeling to be a winning coach!

Wingate pilots at United Airlines (clockwise from left): Lester Tom, Andrew Cummings, Anthony Manswell and Richard A. John. Anthony Manswell was the first of David D. Strachan's students to successfully complete Air Force undergraduate pilot training.

# Chapter Three:
## *The Game*

In my mission to empower young people to achieve success in reaching the goal as a career professional pilot, it was important for me to teach them to understand the game. Many did not understand basic realities, such as segregated housing, where black people do not by chance wind up in special clusters, or ghettos, but get there because of federal policies or white-supremacist practices. Often, these areas are turned over to black people because they consist of old, dilapidated housing and schools. I found that it was not easy to reach the minds of these young people who had been damaged by a white-supremacist educational system. Some of them would call me a racist or prejudiced, to my face or behind my back. Damaged people will attack even the benefactors who attempt to rescue them from a deadly enemy like white supremacy. This is a reality I confronted while carrying out my mission. However, it is pleasing for me to say that, sometimes, perhaps years later, some of these same difficult students came back to the school and told me that what I had said about the omnipresence of the white supremacist system that is in place in the United States of America was true.

Since my retirement from the flight program at Wingate High School on 3 July 1996, some of the program's former students have held a number of reunions. It has been my observation at most of these celebrations that those in attendance were students who had succeeded in landing pilot jobs. Other pilots did not attend because they were not able to take time off from their jobs all over the world. Many of them work in Africa, Asia, the Middle East, and Europe. Some of the others who decided not to become pilots or who redirected or deferred their goals tended not to attend the reunions. I have found that there are many students who completed the pilot-training program at college and decided to pursue another field. Many of them are quite successful. Some of them were diverted from their goal by being recruited into religious organizations where they lost sight of their career plans. At the reunions, we enjoyed being together and we talked about our lives and how we can help others following us in the aviation field.

The Wingate H.S. flight class was created in the early 1970s with a Justice Department grant that was supposed to expose this group of youth to an introduction to pilot training, to encourage them to complete high school, and to encourage them to stay out of the school-to-prison pipeline. This was a time in U.S. history when black pilots were engaged in lawsuits just to get jobs at airline companies. It was an uphill battle, with some victories. It has not ended to this day. It is still a challenge to break the job caste system that has yet to disappear from the aviation field.

To me, all of my students, whom I believe number in the thousands, were special and loved by me. Empowering all of them has always been a joy for me. In this section, I have selected two of them as examples of the greatness of many of them. In the following chapter are the reflections of a small number of the many students or others I have touched through mentoring or counseling.

The first one that comes to my mind is Andrew, who came from a single-parent home. Andrew was raised by his mother and had a passion for becoming an airline pilot. I remember him in the classes I taught, always sitting as close to me as he could during the lesson. He was never late or absent. Andrew soaked up aviation mathematics and other subjects like a dry sponge in a bucket of water. As I got to know more about him, I learned he had three jobs and that he worked seven days a week, after school until midnight and also on weekends. He saved his money for college and went on to attend the school I had recommended.

In college, Andrew excelled. He completed a baccalaureate and master's degree and went on to start working on his Ph.D. During this period, he was able to obtain all the aeronautical experience and FAA certificates he needed to qualify for an airline pilot's position at a small regional airline. He successfully navigated these steppingstones in the aviation industry to reach a major airline, where he is an experienced Boeing 747 pilot today.

During his climb up the aviation ladder to the captain's seat, Andrew developed a number of successful commercial enterprises. Yes, he is also a businessman! He has proven to be one of the most generous persons I know in helping others to become pilots and in empowering his children, along with his wonderful wife. I think of Andrew as the "poster-person" for generosity. He is one of the greatest students I have ever influenced.

The other is Diane. As a teenager in my class, Diane asked if it were possible for her to become an airline stewardess, that is to say, a flight attendant. History tells us that the racist policies of the airline industry prevented black women, and men, from becoming flight attendants or pilots for many years. Ruth Carol Taylor was the first black woman to be hired as a flight attendant in the U.S. (1957). When Diane asked me her question, I told her no, she was not going to be a flight attendant. I said that she was going to be the captain of an airliner.

After that day, she defied her family, who thought it was a crazy idea for a black girl to be a pilot. They told her she could be a nurse. She persisted in aiming for a career as a pilot and did well in my class. Despite her success, the money she was going to use for flight training in college was stolen by a member of her family just before she was to depart for Alabama. This incident did not defeat her in reaching her goal of becoming a professional pilot. Diane took a non-flying job and earned more funds to begin her pilot training. She earned a baccalaureate degree, then spent some time as a teacher in an aviation program at a Queens, New York, high school. She also earned the FAA credentials that qualified her

Wingate graduate Jahvon Tuitt helps organize Black History Month exhibits at Jet Blue Airlines. Here he is flanked by two historical figures, Marcus Garvey and Bessie Coleman, one of America's first female pilots.

Captain Diane Pencil (front row right) with First Officer, Oluranti Ogunwale, and crew flying out of Lagos, Nigeria.

for an entry-level position as a pilot at a regional airline. Today, she has moved forward to the captain's seat on the latest model Boeing 737 airliner. She flies all over Africa for a large Nigerian airline, with additional duties training and managing pilots.

❧❧❧

Over the years that I have been a teacher, my ears have taken in the words of many "educators" who have expressed low expectations for students of color. In one school where I was serving, I overheard a counselor say that a white student did not belong there. She said he belonged in the elite Stuyvesant High School on the basis of his color, that is to say, race. This "counselor" was completely oblivious to the brilliant black students all around her at that school. At another school attended by two of my own children, twins, the principal initially assigned them to a class with struggling students, *i.e.*, students who were behind in grade level. I had to threaten him with legal action to have him make the proper class placement. When my twins got to their new class, I found out that the class was one of mostly white children in a school that was predominately black and Latino. This was a class, I believe, reserved for children of the principal's own demographic. When I saw him again, he looked like a person whose face had turned into an overripe tomato and he was unable to look me in the eye.

The story of the Wingate H.S. pilots is one of students of color rising from the segregated schools of Crown Heights and Bedford-Stuyvesant, both in Brooklyn, and defying the expectations of many people by becoming airline pilots, some of them captains. Some white people have suffered cognitive dissonance, that is, shock, on seeing one of my students at the controls of an airliner. There have been occasions when white people got off the airplane. Many of my former students have been mistaken for "redcaps," *i.e.*, porters, while walking through the terminal in their pilot's uniform.

I believe the successful story of the Wingate H.S. pilots is considered to be an aberration by many people. This is similar to other instances in which black people have achieved high goals. For example, Barack Obama may be president, but real authority is maintained by oligarchs and plutocrats who have not relinquished any control over the levers of power. The greatness of the Wingate pilots is a reason to celebrate, however, we have not yet arrived at a new day where we can actually say that we live in a place of liberty and justice for all.

During my early years and into my twenties, I feel that I did not grasp navigating and surviving in the white-supremacist racism of America. Also, it did not help me to reach my pilot goal when I got the brush-off from the only black pilot I knew, the one in the ROTC program at NYU. It was a figurative, and could possibly have been a literal death for me when I came into contact with southern-style, white-supremacy racism in the Air Force, coupled with the sexual attack on my wife while I was deployed to Japan. I was unable to talk about this rape for many years because of the painful emotional effect it had upon me. I felt helpless in getting justice for Joyce and myself. I felt like I, too, had been raped.

Rape is a crime that takes place on college campuses all the time and is often, these days, highlighted in news reports. Many black women have been subject to sexual assault by the police, who consider them an easy target. My feeling is that, in America, the rape of black women is not regarded as an important issue. All you have to do is think back to the Central Park jogger case, where a number of black boys were arrested for a rape they did not commit. Ditto the Scottsboro Nine case and half a dozen other infamous cases. At the same time, the sexual assault of black women gets scant attention, or the women are ridiculed. I've learned that the prisons are full of a significant number of black people who committed no crime at all, or were not the ones who did commit the crime. Everyday the papers are full of cases where people are exonerated after many years in prison. This "justice" system is, in effect, an injustice system for black people and it is fueled by white supremacy.

Joyce did not go to the police for a reason. The only contact she had had with the police in Nashville, Tennessee, was when she was stopped on a road at night by a white policeman who then attempted to rape her in her car. He did not carry out his intentions only after she told him she had a venereal disease.

It took me a long time to recover from these wounds that I still have to this day. I was able to transform myself, nevertheless, into the type of person that I needed in my life and that I never had. I developed myself into a passionate teacher, counselor and mentor, with the singular mission of empowering young people coming behind me so that they could achieve their highest potential. I feel that my personal tragedies have led to victory for many others.

☜☜☜

*I want to be a pilot!* Over the years, I have heard many people say they wanted to be pilots. I've listened to the words coming out of the mouths of many, many, *many* people, but it's been my experience that most of them don't have a clue about the planning or effort it takes to reach that goal. For most of the people I have met, this was idle talk with no action on their part. At this time, I must talk about some basic things regarding the achievement of the goal of becoming a commercial airline pilot or a pilot for the military.

In 1994, I was appointed director of the Negro Airmen's International (NAI) Summer Flight Academy at Tuskegee University in Alabama. With the help of volunteers, flight instructors and ground instructors, I organized and ran this free program to teach students from all over the country to fly. My policy at Wingate H.S. and at the flight-training institute at Tuskegee was to give every youngster a chance. Many students were able to solo an aircraft and pass the FAA written examination for private pilot credentials while at the academy. Many others, however, decided not to

# Family Portraits

Franklin Rodriguez (l.), his brother
David, mother Angela Acosta, and
son Francisco

Willis Reid and family on vacation

Ewan Duncan with his daughters

Richard A. John and family celebrate the holidays

take advantage of this opportunity to learn to fly in a free program, even after verbalizing their desire to be a pilot. This was an important learning experience for me because I saw the flaw of how some of these young people were selected for this all-expenses-paid program. Adults on those various selection committees did not know how to interview the students. A number of the students were selected because they impressed the members of their local selection committee with high grades. Those committees ignored the fact that the student had no interest in becoming a pilot. Some of them did not take advantage of the flying lessons when they got to Tuskegee because they were afraid to get into an airplane!

When you don't have the funds to pay for pilot training, and you really want to be a pilot, there are several ways you can reach your goal. Here is a list of actions that *should* be taken, not necessarily in this order and not necessarily by everyone, depending on what your particular circumstances are and what your professional goal is:

- Take one or two flight lessons with a local instructor to see if this is what you really want to do.
- Investigate low-cost pilot training programs in small public junior colleges or senior colleges located in the southern part of the United States where the weather tends to favor flying.
- Work toward a baccalaureate degree, a B.S. or B.A., by enrolling in a local public college with low tuition. It does not have to be in aeronautics or anything related to flight technology, although a B.S. in aviation administration will be advantageous should you decide to apply for a management position at an airline in the future. Your degree can be in any field that you find interesting and in which you will graduate in the shortest period of time.
- Another option is to enroll in a public college where you can earn your degree by taking tests, such as CLEP tests,

without having to pay for or attend classes. Many people don't know about this way to get a degree at a very low cost. Don't pay any attention to advertising on television, radio, billboards, etc., for private, profit-making colleges. They are only interested in taking your money.

- Make sure you apply for and get your U.S. citizenship if you are eligible and a non-citizen. Do not delay because delaying it will close the door to numerous opportunities that are not available to non-citizens. Many people are eligible for citizenship and delay applying for it for some reason or another, which is a big mistake. The government makes non-citizens jump through extra hoops before allowing them to take pilot training as a result of the events of 9/11.

- Apply for the best job you know about. If you are eligible for a civil service job such as firefighter, police, Metropolitan Transit Authority (MTA), New Jersey Transit, other civil service job, apply for that job, with benefits. Once you have a good job, you'll be able to save money for funding your pilot training, if you still want to be a pilot by this time. Don't forget that there are age restrictions on flying, especially in the military. Find out what they are and set your goals accordingly.

- Set your priorities! Do you really want pilot training if you buy yourself a new luxury car? Or expensive clothing? Or if you go on luxurious vacations? Think about it.

- Study and pass as many FAA written examinations as you can before you attend flight school.

- If you already have your college degree, investigate the numerous private, accelerated flight programs you can attend where you get all of the FAA credentials in a short period of six months or less, which is fabulous.

- Stay in contact with other pilots who will be happy to reach back and pull you forward. Once you have arrived, you can reach back, you *must* reach back, to do the same for others behind you.

I cannot think of one student who failed to achieve their goal as a pilot who heeded the mentoring voice that I was able to give to them on a regular basis. Some people, young and old, get so distracted by the immediate desire for material things and by social factors, that they are easily sidetracked onto dead end roads leading to nowhere. This was the experience of some of my former students. In some cases, these dead-end-road students earned the same credentials as their classmates who are flying today as captains of Airbus and Boeing jetliners. I am sad for those who went down the wrong road, for whatever reason, but I'm glad for the people who I had an opportunity to counsel only once or twice, by telephone or in person. That was all they needed to get on track and succeed.

In order to become a successful professional pilot, you must be passionate enough to survive all the barriers in place in the United States of America that block a person of color from reaching that goal. You are in a delusional state if you think that the airlines are looking for black people to give them pilot jobs in this white supremacist country. There are many people who will resent, sabotage or mislead you on your path to the cockpit. This does not mean that everyone is the enemy. There are many allies who will help you, but you have to be cautious to never let anyone tell you what you can't achieve.

Many people will put doubts in your mind out of ignorance or to discourage you. They will say things like, "You can't be a pilot if you wear glasses" or "You can't be a pilot if you get airsick." I can't remember the number of times I have met people who were given misinformation, and that misinformation sabotaged their dream of becoming a pilot before they talked to me. For example, I have known cases where individuals injured themselves by undergoing unapproved laser eye surgery to correct their vision before going into the military. They did not check first for safe options. An investigation would have led them to PRK – *photorefractive keratectomy* – a procedure that is approved for military pilots.

There's no one path to becoming a pilot and not all types of training are suitable for every individual. I think it is important to learn as much as possible about the many different types of pilot certifications that are available: fixed wing, rotary wing (helicopter), single-engine and multi-engine, sea and land, instrument ratings, and so on. It is important to research the various paths that lead to the end goal of being a pilot. Many have taken steps that did not benefit them and spent large sums of money on useless endeavors. Many factors must be considered, including your age, what your health situation is (including eyesight), your finances, and the time you have to dedicate to your training. Different timelines can be set up to qualify yourself as a pilot depending upon your family responsibilities and your employment situation. All of these factors and more have to be taken into consideration.

You may also want to consider what part of the country to train in based on weather patterns and how much flight time you will be able to accrue while in school. The type of school you attend, college or fixed based operation or private instructor, are all ways of obtaining the lessons you need to take the FAA examinations and get your credentials. Your plan to becoming a pilot, your particular roadmap, must be tailored to what is best for you. Flight schools are in the business of making money by getting students. The bottom line for every prospective pilot is to do the homework that will allow you to make good decisions about what type of training you are going to get and where. This means you must review materials, study the options and consult people who know the terrain, such as working pilots, so that you don't end up going down a road that wastes your time and your money. Do not fall by the wayside and bring triumph to your enemy.

It is important to know what to do while you are looking for a pilot's job. For example, if you know another pilot who can walk your application into the human resources department of an airline or a corporation, that can be a tremendous asset, to have one of their own employees present your application. Your résumé must be laser sharp and constructed to impress. Do not write more than one page, including separate sections for education, flying time, work record, and awards. Don't leave any gaps in your work record. Don't clutter the page with extra information that gets in the way of those important things I just mentioned. When you are scheduled for an interview, get briefed by the pilot who walked in your application or someone else you can trust who is acquainted with the hiring process at that company, or at least with the interview portion of the hiring process.

You must also know how to dress to make a good impression during the interview. My policy is to coach all potential candidates for a pilot's job to project a conservative, non-threatening image. For male candidates, I would suggest a navy blue or medium gray, single-breasted suit with either two or three buttons, no more, no less. Your suit can have light pin stripes. Wear a single-vent suit or a no-vent suit that fits well. Your shirt should be Brooks Brothers quality or better, a white shirt that is starched and will go well with a gray or blue tie that is not too busy. Shoes should be plain-toed or wing-tipped lace ups that are black and shined well. As a black candidate, I believe you will be better off having no facial hair, such as a beard, mustache, goatee, or long sideburns. Be clean-shaven and get a short haircut.

For female candidates, I would recommend a gray or blue pantsuit with leather shoes that are suitable for handling the foot controls of an aircraft, and no heavy makeup, perfume, or hair longer than shoulder level. Avoid large jewelry, including large earrings and rings that might catch on the controls in the cockpit.

When going to the interview, make sure that you are not late or more than fifteen minutes early. You can use that early time to visit the restroom and check your clothes and paperwork, including your logbook, which you should have with you for the interview.

Learn how to smile and look pleasant. After the interview, I believe it is good to send a short note of thanks to your interviewer for giving you the opportunity to apply for the job.

Remember that you are in a place, many times, where some people do not want you to have that job. They want it for family members or friends or for someone else of their own ethnicity, and they are not happy about seeing you there. Never lose sight that you can still get the job, not necessarily because you are the brightest bulb, *i.e.*, the smartest in the world, but because of those who went ahead and opened the door for you. Do not deceive yourself with the idea that pilot jobs are given based only on merit. Black people and others have collected huge sums of money as a result of lawsuits because of discrimination in the airline industry. For those companies that have paid out, it is just the cost of doing business.

ક્ષ્ક્ષ્ક્ષ

In my celebration of those students who have achieved great things in the racist aviation industry, I have to recognize the nature of America's capitalist and imperialist system that requires the pitting of its people against each other, which is what is done here so that the wealthy can extract the human and land wealth. I must acknowledge that some of my students, while living in abject poverty under America's caste system, see the achievement of their dream of having an aviation career as being beyond imagination. I've heard many white people blame the black victim for lack of personal responsibility, rather than focus on the one and only goal of corporate capitalism, that being whatever works to improve the bottom line, certainly not to create jobs or benefits for the masses of America's people.

Many people in the U.S.A. celebrate lying to themselves. The governance set up by its founders does not lead to government in the interests of people. The idea drummed into each school child's

David D. Strachan accepts an award for his service as a lifeguard at the Colonial Park pool in the late 1940s. To his right is his partner, Monica Rose. Members of the Community Church of New York who attended the ceremony on December 12, 2002 were (back row, center to right): Fay Bennett-Lord, Doris Edwards and Sally Edwards Asiedu; (center row, left to right): Ruby Sills, Maude Jenkins and Nicole Lord; (front row, left to right): Brenda Carpenter Osayim and Christine Burke. The two unidentified children invited themselves to be in the photo.

Journalist Burnard White of radio station WBAI interviews David D. Strachan at his home, October 2010. Mr. White has since departed WBAI.

head about "liberty and justice for all" is a huge lie, as is calling our system a democracy. It makes me believe the adage I have learned about telling a lie often enough and eventually you will get people to believe it.

I believe that everyone should understand the ethos that allows a small group of rich people, *i.e.*, oligarchs and plutocrats, since America's beginning to rule the masses of its people. Ethnic cleansing and genocide, as well as enslavement, was the prescription for the indigenous people whom European settlers called "Indians." For these settlers, bondservants, and various other European groups, as well as the kidnapped and enslaved African people, divide and rule has been the strategy, and still is to this day, to control people in a *faux* democracy. Most people, black and white, who live in the U.S.A. are victims of the founding policy of white supremacy. It is clear to me that with the wealth created by the labor of its population on the stolen land and with the stolen natural resources of the indigenous people, we could all live in a social and economic system that provides justice and freedom for all people.

You are not going to learn about any of this in most schools and colleges controlled by the oligarchs who run the "educational" system, which is really an extended labor training camp. You must be a ferocious reader and listener to truly educate yourself. A system like America's is not set up to usher you into the top paying jobs such as airline pilot or physician if you are a member of one of the subjugated groups, including African Americans. The money that is needed for the social and economic benefit for all its people, no matter what their color is, is allowed to accrue in the hands of America's rulers as they high-five each other "all the way to the bank," all over the world.

For sometime after my retirement from Wingate in 1996, I would make an occasional appearance at the high school to take students to the airport. On 10 September 2001, I had a stroke. I was taken by ambulance to an inferior ghetto hospital that was not equipped to treat patients for stroke. This led to serious damage that has restricted my activities. At that time, the flight program, in aviation parlance, stalled, went into a spiral, and crashed and burned because I was not there to keep it going. My analysis tells me that the community and its political misleaders in no way had a handle on the value of a program like that existing in the so-called "inner city." They did nothing to protect the goldmine that was in their possession. The power to control what goes on in the schools of the black community is ceded to the mayor, the Board of Education (or recently, Department of Education), and the bureaucratic apparatus that make all the decisions in ghetto areas like the one where Wingate H.S. is located, and they ignore the people who, in many cases, do not make a peep. What this whole scenario amounts to is turning our children over to our worst enemy for their education, with zero input from local politicians, parents and community members.

At this point in time, if students, parents and community members want to reinstate the flight program at Wingate H.S., they are going to have to deluge the Mayor of New York City and the Department of Education with letters and petitions, carry out demonstrations, and prod the local politicians into action in order to get what is needed. A future goal must be to put all the public schools into the hands of the people whose children attend those schools, and not under the dictatorship of one person, *i.e.*, a mayor, as is currently the case in New York City in 2015. I have no knowledge of this type of governance going on in wealthy communities or in the suburbs outside of New York City.

There are forces in some communities, like Crown Heights, that are powerful and yet, the same powerful individuals who have taken charge of local school boards in the past do not have any children attending the public schools in that community. To avoid this happening in the future, schools must be governed by the people, including teachers, who have an allegiance to and love for the students in that school. Parents can empower themselves and their children to chart a course to excellence when schools are in their

Strachan family gathering in Connecticut

Strachan family reunion. David D. Strachan's maternal cousin, Clarice Donaldson, is in the back row center in white. To her left is Edward Strachan and cousin Ivy's daughter, Fay Parks. Ivy Parks is in the front row center. To her right is Edward's wife, Madeline. John R. Strachan's son Johnnie is in the back row, extreme left.

hands. Parental power will preclude the school boards from being lulled into apathy and prevent schools from being turned over to private operators, including charter organizations, as is happening in the state of California right now.

Most children's performance is connected to the social and economic factors the children bring along with them when they attend school. The massive attack against teachers in New York City and turning them into scapegoats is part of a corporate plan to privatize public education – training at all levels, for that matter – and turn schools into a source of private profits. *As we speak*, teachers are slowly being relegated to the position of temporary, part-time workers with no benefits and no job security.

The demise of the Wingate H.S. flight program can be reversed. To do this, we must understand the nature of the capitalist, white supremacist system in which we are living. It is a system that is designed to exploit *all* people for the benefit of the rich and powerful oligarchs and plutocrats who run America and most of the world. This exploitation includes the children of black people who live in the U.S.A. The flight program was not organized to benefit the victims of white-supremacy racism by making them pilots. The Wingate community of parents, students and teachers must understand that the successes of the flight program, when it was in effect, was not enough to keep it going. Any attempt to recreate, resurrect or restore a flight technology program would not depend on just class time, hard work, simulators, airplanes, or providing some flying lessons. The greatest success for all students would depend on putting the program into the hands of a teacher who has the technical knowledge, the energy, and most of all, the love, passion and joy for the success of all the students.

Let us get on the road to taking power for all people in the United States of America. The first step is to analyze the way in which the country is controlled and kept in the hands of the rich and powerful. Our system of governance is one that depends on one political entity that has two divisions, the Republican and

Democratic parties, both having the same ruling-class interests.

I believe that most of the people who are in elective office in the U.S.A. are in the pockets of the oligarchs, *i.e.*, the major corporations. We have a façade of democracy, but not true governance by the people, with citizens being allowed to vote only *after* the rulers have selected the candidates. The word "democracy" is mentioned often enough to drill into the heads of most people that it is in effect, which is not true. Our capitalist economy is on steroids and is able to exploit the people more than any other capitalist economy in the world because of our diversity, which allows rulers to play people against each other by "race," ethnicity and religion, in other words, divide and conquer. People need to do what is needed to learn the game that is being perpetrated against them. The fox – the ruling class – is not going to inform you of what he is planning to do to you. Do not forget that the schools and the media are in the control of the fox. People need to think about why they support predatory political parties that do not operate in their interests and are run by their worst enemies. Many of our people appear to be blind with their eyes wide open, and/or brain-dead in terms of the way they operate.

Since 11 September 2001, many things have changed, including who is allowed to take flying lessons. I would be unable today, in 2015, to provide lessons to some of my Wingate students because they were not yet U.S. citizens while in high school. This would be a major impediment to the operation of my mission. It would be like closing the door of opportunity for students who were immigrants. White people often conveniently forget that their ancestors were immigrants. As I see it, America's citizens are being kept on a short leash, with many black people targeted for criminalization marking them with a stigma that follows them for the rest of their lives. At the same time, neo-liberal policy is turning over government services, including jails and prisons, to private for-profit enterprise.

The bottom line of my life has been to recover from the tragedy of my racist Air Force experience, as well as the sexual assault of my wife while I was stationed overseas. Joyce never recovered from the attack and died early. I feel that my own recovery from these tragedies has motivated me as a teacher, as a counselor, as a coach, and as a human being. My life's work has been to assist young people in getting the information and skills they need to be able to compete in America's white-supremacist racist environment. Some students who were tutored by me have reached back and are helping others behind them. I feel that my personal tragedies have been turned into victories for those I have touched. With my guidance, a number of the young people whom I mentored were able to survive and graduate from Air Force pilot training. I salute them and I celebrate their success. It gives me great joy and a feeling of redemption from the tragedies I experienced early in my life.

In addition, I was able to see all three of my consanguine children achieve doctoral degrees on their way to professional careers. The colleges they attended included Harvard, Hunter, Howard, Yale, Brown, Columbia and Pace, as well as the Sorbonne in Paris. Davia, my first child, from the time she was a little girl, was always interested in people's teeth; she was a natural dentist. She chose to become a pediatric dentist and has served as a clinical professor at a dental college. David, Jr., my son, chose to be a lawyer. His practice specializes in criminal defense. My younger daughter, Dina, decided to be a physician. She is a Board-certified dermatologist with a private practice and serves as a clinical professor at a medical school.

As I think about how I would describe myself, what comes to mind is being a warrior for justice for all people and a tactician for teaching others how to survive the enemy, which is the doctrine and practice of white supremacy, while helping those who are behind to get ahead. This type of behavior will help win some battles.

David D. Strachan and Monica Rose on vacation
in Costa Rica, 2003

David D. Strachan and best friend, the late Leo Downes

All of us must be aware that the enemy is in charge. Know what his goal is and what his plans for you are, that is, know the game, or die in many ways an ignorant fool.

# Part II:
## *My Triumphant Victory*

# Chapter Four:
## *The Pilots Speak*

It is very sad how, in our community, the oligarchs do what they want. If black people were on the case, there would be no way they could have ended a program like this. As long as you allow the people in power to do what they want, they're not going to train black youngsters to do the type of things I was training them to do. We have a large community of African descent, and we stand by while those in power dismantle our most productive programs or sabotage those programs with non-caring staff and outdated equipment. Politicians decide it's a failing school and are willing to discontinue an excellent program, and most of the time, people who live in that community don't even know what's going on.

I decided to include in my memoir the experience of many of those who I mentored over the years. You will see, as you read this section, that some did not initially want to be pilots. Others earned all the credentials and changed their minds about being in aviation. They chose other paths. I did not exclude those who stumbled along the way and got involved with the legal system.

Many of the pilots who benefited from the Wingate-Strachan support system are active in reaching out and throwing a lifeline to other pilots of color who are wounded or damaged by the unending program of white-supremacy racism that has never stopped,

Opposite: Wingate-Strachan pilots gather for a reunion at the brownstone home of David D. Strachan in Bedford-Stuyvesant, Brooklyn, October 2010. Pictured front row, left to right, are: Malcolm Bennett (a student from AATC), Esan Baptiste (also a student from AATC), David D. Strachan, Ian Abraham, Anthony Manswell. Second row, left to right: Jim Bob Jones, Jason Matthews, Steven Smith, O'Neil Barnes, O'Neil Soares. Third row, left to right: Charles Tai, Wayne Brown, Ewan Duncan. Fourth row, left to right: Leaford Daley, an unidentified individual, Richard A. John, an unidentified individual. Last row, left to right: Marlon Reynolds, an unidentified individual, Antonio Smith. Several pilots who attended the reunion had departed by the time this photograph was taken.

in aviation and elsewhere. A whole book could be written just on the sabotage done by people who don't see black pilots as being in their place.

I look forward to our next reunion because it is always a joy to see many of my former students, talk with them about old times, and find out what they're doing now. Read on...

Richard A. John

My name is RICHARD A. JOHN ("Raj") and I was a student in the Aerospace Technology Department at George W. Wingate High School in Brooklyn, New York. I migrated from Trinidad, West Indies to Brooklyn in the summer of 1980, and that fall I joined the flight program at Wingate. I was a student of Mr. Strachan during those memorable high school years. The program was under the leadership of Mr. Strachan and he was the primary driver that empowered many students to move forward and capture our dreams of becoming aviators.

I can firmly state without reservation that Mr. Strachan provided the required mental skill set and aeronautical knowledge that was necessary to leave my home in East Flatbush, Brooklyn, and venture one thousand miles to a little-known flight school deep in the heart of Alabama. It was 1983; I was seventeen years old with a one-way ticket on a Greyhound bus, a duffel bag, and a dream….

Flight school was a challenge, but, despite the odds, many of Mr. Strachan's students, including myself, earned our aeronautical credentials at that school in Alabama. We were then channeled into undergraduate school in what became known as the academic triangle: Wingate H.S., Alabama Aviation and Technical College, and St. Francis College in Brooklyn. Later on, I went on to graduate school. The important point to note is that after high school, Mr.

Strachan did not stop providing the required support that we all need from time to time. Mr. Strachan mentored us through flight school and beyond. There were no boundaries: he was always a phone call away. Needless to say, his style of teaching and mentoring was rather unusual, even out of the box. Many of his students viewed him as unconventional and borderline eccentric, but eccentric in a loving and kind manner. The only satisfaction he got from his investment in his students was to revel in their successful achievement of a dream!

As I reflect on his teaching style, if you were a student in his aerospace technology class, you did not get just a lesson in aerodynamics, meteorology, or Federal Aviation Administration regulations. In addition to learning the required aviation-related topics, Mr. Strachan lectured on global politics and how "we" fit into the grand scheme of things. His lectures would catapult your mind into believing in your own potential greatness. Those were his finest moments that set him apart from all my professors, past and present. He always had the capacity to deliver more than a simple classroom experience.

Writing this short message is difficult for me because it cannot give a fair or adequate account of Mr. Strachan's accomplishment with respect to his impact on aviation, and more specifically, African American aviation. There were three aviation-related high schools providing pilot training in New York City in the 1980s: George W. Wingate in Brooklyn, Park West in Manhattan, and August Martin in Queens. It is my belief that Wingate produced exponentially more pilots than these two other high schools combined, primarily because we were fortunate at Wingate to have the guidance and leadership of Mr. Strachan.

For the past twenty-two years I have been a pilot for United Airlines based out of New York City and I am currently the captain of an Airbus-320. I am also a member of the adjunct faculty in the College of Aeronautics at Embry-Riddle Aeronautical University in Florida. My story is not unique: Mr. Strachan touched hundreds of students during his tenure at Wingate. Many moved forward to become airline, corporate or military pilots working in many different countries and companies, including Emirates Airlines in Dubai, U.A.E.; ARAMCO in Saudi Arabia; Africa, China, the Caribbean, and so on. I live in Brooklyn with my wife and three kids, always thankful for having had the opportunity to experience life with a true mentor to keep me on my path.

Capt. "Raj" John

Some advice from Captain John on becoming a professional pilot:

- Develop a strategy early in life to attain the goal of capturing a pilot job.

- Don't limit your dream to simply learning how to fly an aircraft, but earn your academic credentials in order to build upon the dream of becoming a pilot.

- Seek out resources to finance getting your flight and academic credentials.

- Build a network of aviation mentors and individuals who have achieved success in their careers. Reach out and solicit their input and advice prior to making important decisions.

- Finally, pursue your goal with a relentless passion that can overcome any and all obstacles.

O'Neil Barnes

O'NEIL GARTH BARNES was born in Jamaica on August 16, 1970. Like several of his colleagues who graduated from Wingate High School, O'Neil believes that he would be working as a pilot today regardless of where he had attended high school. He says, "We're all pretty close, just as a result of our experiences from school and even more so when we got to college." Did having David D. Strachan as a mentor have anything to do with that closeness? "Absolutely. That was, in essence, the foundation. The whole experience of going to Wingate, of meeting new friends, provided me with another family, another parent, from the time that I entered Wingate and embarked on this journey."

O'Neil was raised by his grandmother, Myrines Jones, and an uncle in Jamaica in a home that was relatively strict. The most important thing that his uncle taught him, he says, was that *education is the key*. "I was four years old when my mom left Jamaica and I remember my grandmother taking me to the airport to see my mom leave. She couldn't bring me here at that time. I remember I was hugging my grandmother's leg and crying when my mom climbed the stairs to go into the airplane. It was back in the old days and you could go to the observation gallery. Maybe five minutes after she got on the airplane, I totally forgot about her because now my focus was on the airplane. The noise kind of freaked me out, so I was still holding my grandmother's leg, but now I'm looking at the airplane and I was intrigued by it. And that was it; it stayed with me." O'Neil says that even at four he had a good awareness of time, so every day after his mother's departure, at about the same time, he'd look up in the sky and he'd see an airplane flying. "It would be, in essence, the same flight that my mom left on."

He moved to the United States when he was thirteen and despite his age, his mom sent him to a babysitter after school because she was terrified of leaving him in the house alone. "But I had discipline so ingrained in me that that [bad behavior] wasn't something I had an inclination to be a part of." He graduated with honors from junior high school and, because he knew he wanted to fly, applied for admission to August Martin and Park West High Schools. He ended up going to Wingate, his zoned school, ostensibly because of 'geography.' He did not know at the time that Wingate had an aviation program. "I have an older cousin who went to Wingate and what I remember about the school was all the bad [news] that I heard from my cousin: fights, shootings, all that good stuff. I was like, 'Ah, man, I'm forced to go here,' but then I found out they had a flight program and I was actually looking forward to it."

David D. Strachan was the chairman for the aviation department, he remembers. "Bro. Strachan caught my attention because he reminded me so much of my Uncle Basil in Jamaica, just in how serious he was about education. We used to have these permission slips that we'd get, probably Wednesday and have to turn it in by Thursday in order to fly the following Tuesday. He would come around and he would hand out the slips and if you didn't get one, you weren't going flying. He was very serious about it.

"A lot of the guys thought that he was only interested in what you were doing in his class," O'Neil says, "but what he would do was to speak to the other teachers and check your progress in their classes. And it wasn't only about schoolwork; it was about your participation, your punctuality, your tests, your appearance, and also if you were respectful of the teacher. It was definitely the whole-person concept, and that reminded me so much of my upbringing. A lot of guys would ask, 'Bro. Strachan, how come I didn't get a permission slip?' and he would tell them, 'You know you're not doing the right thing.' Some guys were rebellious because they didn't see the seriousness of how he took his job. From his experiences, he tried to impart that seriousness on us to insure that we were successful in what it was we were about to embark on."

At the time, what David D. Strachan was teaching, another former student, Anthony Manswell, was living. "[Anthony] was older than a few of us, a different year group, but he would come back to the school periodically and talk to us, and it reinforced what Bro. Strachan was saying because Anthony was from the Islands, also. I remember him coming in in his flight suit and sitting down and talking to us about the experiences of going through pilot training, you know, sitting in the bathroom with a plunger and 'chair-flying,' going through the maneuvers in his head, and I kept saying to myself, 'Wow, he sounds just like me. He actually came here [from Jamaica] and sat in this class with this teacher, and here he is in pilot training for the Air Force.' It created the perfect mentorship, having Bro. Strachan teach the theory and then having Anthony provide an example of a way to get to where it was that we wanted to be."

After graduating from Wingate in 1988, O'Neil and a few of his classmates took the advice of David D. Strachan and attended Alabama Aviation and Technical College (AATC). "I was so committed to what it was I wanted to do that I called the school and made arrangements to go down there before actually graduating, just to get the lay of the land and see what it was I was going to partake. I'd saved some money and bought my own plane ticket, but I needed consent from my mom because I was underage and I needed to get a hotel room." He went down with two classmates and as he remembers, "My mom was a little 'pensive' I guess would be the word because of the history of the South, you know..." Unlike many mothers, however, O'Neil's mom did not try to dissuade him.

In August, O'Neil, his cousin and two classmates packed up the car that his uncle had given him and drove from New York to Alabama. The college was so small, they hadn't yet addressed the issue of housing female students and his two classmates were young women. "So we ended up getting an apartment, Diane, Carlean and I. I had a car, so I provided transport for everybody until other people started coming in with cars. It was great. There were times when we'd get money from our parents and we'd put it in our flight accounts so we could fly, then pay the bills and after that, we'd have maybe twenty or thirty bucks in our pocket that might have to last for a month. A lot of times it was honey buns and Mountain Dew for lunch. I really learned a lot, not only about flying, but also in terms of how human beings should live. To this day, most of the guys are closer than brothers. If there's something going on in my life where I'm feeling down, I can always call one of those guys and talk to them and they're like, 'Hey, don't worry about it, I've been through that.' It's a bond I don't think will ever be broken."

O'Neil graduated from AATC in 1990 and during a visit home, his cousin with whom he had grown up in Jamaica was violently killed. He'd had every intention of returning to Alabama and becoming a flight instructor, but his cousin's sudden death at age twenty-two rerouted his plans. "I ended up staying in New York. I wasn't able to focus on what it was that I wanted to focus on. I stayed out of school for a semester and then I enrolled in college." O'Neil earned his B.A. from St. Francis College in Brooklyn in 1993.

Despite his upbringing and his own internal sense of discipline, O'Neil acknowledges the influence that David D. Strachan has had on his life. "Bro. Strachan created, in a nutshell, the roadmap. It was not necessarily a map that everybody had to follow, but it gave us the tools. If you didn't want to follow the example that was set, say, by Anthony Manswell, just to be able to seek people out, to seek out information to create your own roadmap [was helpful]. For the guys who didn't follow the path which [Bro. Strachan] pointed out, not that they weren't successful, but a lot of times it was a lot more difficult just because it was something that was tried and tested. As long as you were willing to put in the work, you'd definitely be able to get from point A to point B.

"Now, whenever I have the opportunity, I go back into the public schools and talk to kids because I think it's important," says O'Neil. "As kids, we're not locking in on the idea of what it is we want to do. I think what happens a lot of times is, it's just like leaving your house. You never leave your house saying, 'Well, I'm just going to go somewhere,' not having any idea where. As kids we have an idea where we are and where it is we want to go. Where we lose a lot of kids is: there's no way of connecting the two. I think Bro. Strachan basically created the map that connected the two."

O'Neil remembers one particular incident that happened while he was a student at AATC. Ironically, the incident did not happen in Alabama. As part of the curriculum, students had to make solo cross-country flights, including planning the trip, to develop their navigational skills. He and a buddy planned this particular trip in single-engine airplanes, "an overland hike," he says, from Ozark, Alabama to Orlando, Florida. The plane was not equipped to fly over water.

"So we landed at Orlando Executive Airport and typically what happens is you land, you go to the fixed base operator because you're going to buy gas, and usually they have a courtesy car so that you can go get something to eat. So we landed and there we were, two young African American men, and we went and spoke to the folks at the counter to ask for a courtesy car. And they're like, 'O.K., just hold on a second.' So we're waiting. Another crew came in, I don't know from where, but they didn't look like us. They went up and asked for a car and the person took the key off [the hook] and gave it to them. So we went back and asked for a car again and the same thing happened, again. So then they finally got around to asking for a driver's license. My friend Brian took out his and gave it to them. Well, his driver's license, like many of ours, just from being in and out of your wallet, looked worn. They called the police because they were like, 'Well, this looks like somebody tried to alter it.' So, they didn't want to give us a car and now we're like, all right, fine. We both sensed what was going on and decided let's get out of here. We went out to our airplanes and we were getting ready to do our pre-flight checks and over comes this cop. He's like, 'Can I see the papers for the airplane?' He kind of let into Brian a little and then came over to me, and same thing, so I said something like, 'Listen, I'm not trying to be disrespectful, but the school told us if we ever got ramp-checked'—because periodically the FAA does that—'to tell the agent where the paperwork is on the airplane. You can look at it, but I'm not allowed to take it out and give it to you.' So then he asked for my driver's license and then it turned into this really nasty thing where he was trying to get us mad. I stood my ground. I told him, 'Listen, I don't know what's going on, and I don't know why your disposition is the way it is, but just understand that we might be two black kids, but we're here with the support of the State of Alabama. On the back of the airplane it says Alabama Aviation and Technical College, which is an accredited school that is funded partly by the State. They own and operate this airplane and whatever it is that happens to us, the school is going to know about it and the State is going to know about it. So whatever it is that you think you're going to do, you can go ahead and do it, but just understand that we're part of a school and they know we're here.' He didn't like that. I think he realized we hadn't done anything wrong, so he cursed at us and told us to get into our airplanes and get the blink-blink out of there. It was funny because I thought I would have experienced that kind of thing in Alabama, which I never did." In fact, O'Neil says his first month or so in Alabama was *weird* because, walking down the street, strangers would say hello and wave. "We were from New

York and we were not accustomed to that kind of behavior, so we're looking around to see who they're waving at.

"Bro. Strachan told us that there were going to be a lot of instances where people would try to bait [us] into positions where they push buttons, so if you get upset, you start getting disrespectful and cursing, and that's grounds for them to do what it is they want to do. I remember guys going through the class at Wingate. Bro. Strachan would sit them down and try to school them on this stuff, and they just rebelled. I could never understand that because, for me, he was a godsend. He had our well-being at the forefront. A lot of the lessons that we learned from him in high school, just being able to talk to people, to articulate, definitely came in handy."

It was a source of inspiration, says O'Neil, that David D. Strachan was African American. "I can't remember if he was out on medical leave, but we had some other teachers at one point who administered the program and it wasn't the same. They just didn't show his sense of urgency. They didn't show the interest in us as students. He'd tell us stories about when he was in the military and had to use a separate gate and stuff like that, and those things resonated with us. He had a lot of credibility from his experiences and from the fact that he looked like us.

"By the time I got to Wingate and became a student of Bro. Strachan's, what I got from him totally reinforced what my grandmother had taught me. Even from birth, my grandmother was around. That's the person who was my caretaker. I remember when she sat us down one day and said, 'If you don't have any money, if you have manners and you're respectful of people, you'll travel the world many times over.' To this day, I've yet to prove her wrong." Myrines Jones eventually moved to the U.S. because of her failing health. She passed away in 2011. "It was difficult for me because I wanted to repay her and I felt that I never did. Before she passed, she told me, 'You already have. I remember the day we went to the airport. I remember when it was that you had this idea that you wanted to fly.' I think now about where I am in life and what it is that I've achieved, and minus her and my uncle, I would not be here talking to you."

Nevertheless, O'Neil admits, "If you peel the onion back a couple of layers, I guess I have benefited from the efforts of many people. When I joined the Air National Guard, the demographics of the Guard in New York State didn't reflect the community. As a result, there was a huge push to find qualified minority pilots. They were like, 'Well, we can't find [black] people who meet the qualifications to go to pilot training,' and the flag was waved: you guys are not looking!"

According to O'Neil, there were recruiters who were put in place to screen people. "You had to have a four-year degree. Flight time wasn't something that was required, but it was highly advantageous to have. And then you had to take the AFOQT [Air Force Officers Qualifying Test], which was kind of an armed services vocational aptitude battery that sampled different areas of your knowledge. You'd have an overall score and then you'd have scores in each discipline: reasoning, comprehension, math, etc. For aviation, you had to have good scores in certain areas and that's where a lot of people get tripped up, because not having been exposed to aviation, that part of the test would definitely be a limiting factor for them. So having the aviation background allowed me to excel in this portion of the test."

In July 2016, O'Neil will have served twenty years with the Air National Guard. He became a traditional part-timer in the Guard, flying on his days off, when he joined Continental Airlines in 2005. He is now at United Airlines as a result of the merger between Continental and United. In the footsteps of David D. Strachan, he now reaches out to other young men who are trying to overcome the obstacles placed in their path on the way to becoming professional pilots.

Ruel Lindsay

RUEL (pronounced *ru-el*) LINDSAY confesses that one of his biggest regrets in life will be that he did not listen to David D. Strachan. "I'm not what you'd consider one of Mr. Strachan's success stories. I'm one of the few that didn't fully follow his advice."

Ruel was bitten by the flying bug as a boy growing up in Jamaica. "We often had family members come from overseas, so we had to go out to the airport to pick them up or see them off. There was something about airplanes. As a boy only 'yay' high [he makes a motion with his hand], I'm looking at these jumbo jets through the railing of the balcony—they seemed like bars to me—and waving to the people on the plane, assuming they could see us. We assumed we could see them, too." He was seven or eight years old when he took his first flight from Kingston to Montego Bay and back.

Fourteen when he came to the United States, Ruel had already finished Third Form, the academic equivalent of tenth grade, but they put him in ninth grade anyway. "There were only two things I wanted to do," he says, "either fly or be a carpenter. The desire was just somewhere there in the 'mishmosh' of the brain." In a twist of fate or policy or both, Ruel did not find out about the flight technology program at Wingate High School until the latter part of his senior year, and that is when he met Mr. Strachan. "I thought it was really bizarre because, when you start at the school, they ask you what field you're interested in and the only three programs I was offered were medical science, law and business. There would have been no reason to be in any other program had I known about flight technology." He graduated from Wingate in 1984 and attended the State University of New York in Farmingdale (SUNY/Farmingdale) on the advice of a guidance counselor, despite the fact that David D. Strachan had recommended Alabama Aviation and Technical College (AATC) for his pilot's license. "I already had all my gears set for SUNY/Farmingdale," he says.

After a year at Farmingdale and never even seeing an airplane until the end of that year ("because their program was more theoretical than practical"), Ruel decided that he needed to go back and talk to Mr. Strachan. "He repeated his original advice, adding, 'If you'd followed my advice the first time, you'd already have your license.' I transferred to AATC in December 1985 and I was in an airplane on Day Two of the program. Within one month, I had my private pilot's license. I was fortunate to be directed to the proper school by Mr. Strachan to get my flight training. Mr. Strachan is very direct and he makes sure that whatever leaves his mouth is truth. If you follow his advice, you will see the fruit of your labor."

Thirty years after meeting Mr. Strachan in high school, Ruel says that he still talks to him and seeks his advice. "The most important thing that he did for me was to steer me towards truth, and he's been doing that since Day One when he told me where to go to school. The one thing he's always said was, '*Brother Rule*,'" and here Ruel mimics the deep baritone voice of David D. Strachan along with the mispronunciation of his own name, "'*Brother Rule, you can do anything you want,*' and then he would add, '*as long as you put your mind to it!*'" Ruel adds regretfully, "That's what he basically exposed in my character. It was this lack of focus that cost me a flying career. But he's always reached out to me. I have a son and Mr. Strachan always asks about him, ever since birth. I think he's influenced how I father my children. While I don't know if my son is getting all this, I am passing on wisdom that I have learned from Mr. Strachan and I know he's getting something. My father is alive and well, and I consult with him, also, so it's not like I don't have a dad."

Ruel has held several corporate positions during his career, including as a graphic artist and an insurance salesman. "I'm not one of [David D. Strachan's] success stories, at least, not in the field of aviation, but I do consider myself a successful person in terms of being a man, especially a black man."

*A Tribute to David D. Strachan*

Mr. Strachan is a beacon of truth,
innate power, indignant purpose, and a dogged
perseverance, aimed like a laser
of righteous love at the hearts
of wayward young men,
such as was the one whom this pens.

It is that love laser with which
he incises away at the cancers
of sloth and misguided notions
that infect the hearts of young men,
robbing them of themselves.

He is a tireless crusader for young black men,
Ever-seeking to free them from the proverbial
yoke of prejudice and latent self-hatred.

He is my mentor, and, if I'm worthy, he is my friend.

Ruel D. Lindsay

Anthony Manswell

If David D. Strachan has been a father figure to many of the students he taught in high school or mentored beyond high school, then WAYNE ANTHONY MANSWELL has been, as one of his fellow Wingate pilots calls him, *'The Godfather'* of us all.

"I credit Mr. Strachan with helping me to live my dream, and not only that, I owe my career to him," says Anthony, the first of David D. Strachan's Wingate scholars to make it through undergraduate pilot training in the U.S. Air Force. With a career that spans more than twenty-five years with United Airlines and fourteen years of service in the Pennsylvania Air National Guard, where he flies the A-10 fighter jet, Captain Anthony Manswell says it was "the Good Heavens" that sent him to Wingate High School, his zoned school, especially since his mother, fearing Wingate's reputation for being pretty rough at the time, wanted him to go to South Shore.

One of the things Anthony appreciates most about David D. Strachan is the guidance that he gave to all his students. "We had no clue about aviation, so him saying, 'Go to this school; don't go to that school,' was critical."

David D. Strachan had his students at Wingate order a pamphlet listing aviation schools nationwide that were governed by Part 141 of the Federal Aviation Administration (FAA) regulations. These were state-funded schools where flight instructors were paid by the state, not by the student taking the lesson. Anthony takes credit for being the person who 'discovered' Alabama Aviation and Technical College (AATC) under the tutelage of David D. Strachan. "He was the one who told us about those schools. We wrote to the FAA, got the handbook, and then he told us, 'You don't want to stay in the Northeast. Go to warm places like Florida, Texas and Arizona. You want to be flying on a daily basis.' Students who didn't follow his advice went to New Hampshire and they didn't fly. They didn't get their licenses at the rate that we did because of snow. So I asked him, 'Well, Alabama is the first state on the list. How about Alabama?' He said, 'Yeah, it's warm down there, too, depending on what part of Alabama.'

"So those were crucial points, attending a state college versus a private college where you have to pay for the airplane and the instructor, so your rates are much higher, maybe $100 per hour. We sent out, I think, eight or ten letters to those colleges. One or two in Florida responded, Arizona, and also AATC. They were the cheapest. They were in our ballpark. What we came to understand was what Mr. Strachan was trying to explain about Part 141. Rates at AATC were $20 per hour at that time, which paid for the airplane, the instructor, the fuel, everything. So for every $100, we flew five times as much as the students who went to private schools. We built up our hours."

Born in Trinidad and Tobago, Anthony was eleven when he came to the United States. He attended Winthrop J.H.S. in Brooklyn and graduated from Wingate H.S. in 1982. He spent the next four years in Alabama, first as a student at AATC, then staying on as a flight instructor while attending Troy State University where he earned his bachelor's degree in 1986. After graduating, he flew with a small commuter airline, Continental Express, for a year and a half while simultaneously working through the process of getting into the Air National Guard. Once in the Guard and with enough flight time under his belt, Anthony applied for a position at United

Airlines at the age of twenty-five.

"My first huge '*Ah, ha!*' moment regarding Mr. Strachan's tutelage was when I got hired at United," says Anthony, when he discovered during orientation that the average age of their pilot trainees was forty-four years old. "That's when it really brought it home to me that, based on the guidance he gave us, we were able to make a quantum leap... That showed me how powerful the information was." He says it was a couple of things that allowed him and others to make this quantum leap.

"A lot of people think, 'Hey, I'll do this on the side initially, then eventually I'll get what I want.' I think, from his guidance, we became super-focused." He likens the aspiration to become a pilot to being in a boxing ring. "Once you're in the fight, you don't take time out to understand what's going on around you. The reason you have a coach is because you might be thinking you're doing something, but you're not. The coach says, '*Keep your hands up!*' and you're thinking you already have your hands up. By getting Mr. Strachan's guidance at an early age, I was able to get hired sooner, so most of the co-pilots and flight attendants I fly with, especially when I fly to Europe as captain on the Boeing-767/757, are older than I am."

Anthony says that he was one of the few in the initial group, himself, Richard John, Lester Tom, Andrew Cummings and others, who had always wanted to fly in the military in addition to flying for an airline. He credits David D. Strachan with helping him achieve this dream at a very early age. "He was highly instrumental in me also becoming a fighter pilot. I had the great fortune of doing both because he referred me to a friend of his, Major General James T. Whitehead."

A retired two-star general, Major General Whitehead was the first African American pilot to fly a U-2 for the U.S. Air Force. He served first in the Air Force and then in the Air National Guard. "When I told Mr. Strachan my interest, he put me in touch with then Colonel Whitehead. He was the one who gave me the breakdown on how the military works and introduced me to the Guard. Like most Americans, I had never even heard of the Air National Guard at that time."

Anthony was not so sure he wanted to join the Guard until Colonel Whitehead told him that he himself flew for an airline (the now-defunct TWA) and served in the Guard on his days off. Anthony was shocked to learn that a person could do both. He was sold on the idea and spent the next year and a half working with Colonel Whitehead until he got a slot in the Pennsylvania Air National Guard along with his mentor. "Awesome gentleman," says Anthony, "friend of Mr. Strachan."

It was Colonel Whitehead who informed Anthony that he should take the Air Force Officer Qualifying Test (AFOQT). At the time, he was planning to transfer to Troy State University in Alabama to obtain his bachelor's degree because Troy State would give him credit for the AATC aviation program, so he made the forty-minute trip to Troy to find out if he could take the AFOQT there. "I went into the ROTC Dept. and I said, 'Hey, I'm from Brooklyn. I heard about this AFOQT, and I need to take this test.'" A man who identified himself as the detachment commander told Anthony that the test took place every third Saturday of the month, and since he had already missed it, he'd have to come back the following month. No problem, said Anthony. He asked if there was a study guide for the test and the detachment commander assured him that there was none, that he would have to rely on what he learned in school.

At that time, Troy State University leased hours from AATC to have some of their ROTC cadets, all of them white, learn to fly. One of the cadets was assigned to an African American instructor who was several classes ahead of Anthony's group at AATC. It was summertime and very hot and humid in southern Alabama. The cadet got sick and threw up in the plane. The instructor brought him down and got him back on the bus to Troy, but in the melee, the cadet forgot his books. So the instructor brought the books to the dorm and asked to leave them there until the white student could come back and get them. "I was there and I said, 'Hey, let me take a look at that stuff.' So I looked through the pile and there was an aerodynamics book and some Air Force ROTC training stuff with a letter that said, 'Dear Cadet: Now that you're a junior in college, you have to make a decision on your Air Force career. We highly suggest you take the Air Force Officer Qualifying Test. Here are the five study guides you need to obtain before you take the test.' The letter was signed by the detachment commander."

Being a New Yorker and young and full of testosterone, Anthony went to the business office and made a copy of the letter. "I got the books and studied. A couple of months later, I went back to Troy to take the test. The detachment commander, the same guy who told me there was no study guide, looked at me and said, 'You look familiar.' It took everything in my body not to knock him out. I think if I had pressed the issue, it might not have gone well for me. Once again, I credit Mr. Strachan with that."

That encounter with the ROTC detachment commander was only one of many race-based incidents along the way, including a hilarious incident involving two students at AATC who dressed up in Ku Klux Klan robes in an attempt to intimidate the boys from New York into sitting in the back row to watch T.V.: it didn't work. But virtually every experience that Anthony Manswell had while climbing the ladder to aviation success reminded him of some lesson he had learned from David D. Strachan in high school. His experience at undergraduate pilot training in the military mirrored that of Lieutenant Strachan's forty years earlier. Many of the white guys in training were way ahead because they grew up in families where dads, uncles and granddads had pilot licenses and some of them owned their own airplanes. Even though he was flying for the Air National Guard, Anthony was required to train with Air Force Academy graduates who had experience flying gliders as cadets. "You go in there thinking, 'Man, these guys are great!' But because of some of the stuff Mr. Strachan was telling us, 'Fly as much as you can. Get all your licenses so you can compete with those guys,' etc., you start understanding that they're ahead because they've been practicing for three or four years already, and it's like anything else: If you practice on this airplane, you can move to another and learn how to fly it. That's one of the things I tell guys when I mentor them for the military. I try to bridge the gap with that knowledge so that they understand what's going on."

Anthony tries to pass on Mr. Strachan's message to a younger generation of pilots, but the end result is not always a good one. "When I talk to kids today, I tell them how powerful information is, that when you get the correct guidance, you get through the maze so much more quickly. Many kids think they accomplish what they have accomplished because they're lucky, and I tell them that 'luck' comes from Laboring Under Correct Knowledge. If you labor under incorrect knowledge, the results are not going to be successful." Anthony also stresses being prepared, as did David D. Strachan to his students, and often introduces the formula, Preparation plus Opportunity equals Success, when working with young people.

"Before going to Alabama, [David D. Strachan] already had us taking FAA written examinations, which was unheard of, especially in an inner-city school. A lot of us in the first group, six or eight of us, went down there with anywhere from one to three written exams already passed. When they spoke to us on the phone, everything was fine, 'Come on down,' but when we showed up, the initial reaction was, 'Are you guys here for the auto mechanics program?' Once that was straightened out and we were redirected to the flight program, it took several weeks before we could convince the instructors that we didn't need to take courses that were designed to teach us how to pass tests. They're explaining to us that it's going to take x-amount of months to do private, x-amount to do commercial, and so on, and some of us raised our hands and said, 'We have those already,' and showed them our scores. They were all highly taken aback. It took them a while to process. There were a couple of other African Americans in the class, but they weren't as serious as we were, so they were in the program for most of two years. Guys like us who had the *focus* from Mr. Strachan, we were already ahead when we arrived.

"Mr. Strachan warned us, 'They're not going to be happy campers when they see you because they're not expecting African Americans. They're not going to be happy that you guys have already passed your private, commercial and instrument written exams.' He also told us, 'They're going to make up all kinds of rules on the spot,' and they did."

Anthony well remembers one such rule change that affected all of them personally and could have been a disaster. Their flight account minimum balance started out at $500, which apparently it had been for a long time. "The program was self-paced, and the guys from New York were moving through it at a fairly good clip, more quickly than the white guys who would fly one day, then take the next day off," he remembers. When the school administrators noticed this, they decided to put the breaks on the rapid pace with which the New York guys were getting their licenses. They arbitrarily raised the flight account minimum to $1000, which, Anthony says, would clearly be a hardship for poor kids from the inner city. "But we called our moms, grandmothers, uncles, and did whatever we had to do to meet the new requirement." Within weeks, the minimum requirement jumped to $1500, then $2000. "And we're saying, 'Wow! At $20 per hour, you're looking at a lot of flying!' So we flew less, and they raised it again to $2500! That's when the white guys started crying. They couldn't afford it either, so the school had to back down. That's one of the things Mr. Strachan had explained to us at Wingate: 'There's going to be a lot of adjustments when you guys show up,' but because of his mentoring, we had that open-mindedness, that understanding, so we weren't in a surprise-mode all the time. I find the kids today, when they tell me about rule changes, I have to remind them that I told them this was going to happen."

Anthony has many nicknames amongst his fellow pilots and another one is 'The Doorman.' "One of my passions has been to get others who are interested into aviation," he says, "so what I did was go back to Wingate, talk to O'Neil Barnes and all those guys and explain to them the process, the tests, the study guides, just about everything." Anthony would visit the high school in the early days wearing his military uniform, and on national holidays he would fly over AATC in his fighter jet and then meet with the students afterwards. He has mentored dozens of younger African American and Latino men and women and helped them get pilot training in the military and/or pilot positions in the airline industry. One young man at Jet Blue Airlines whom he recently tutored said of him, "Anthony doesn't just open the door; he kicks the door down!"

"It comes from an early fascination that I had as a child. When I was five or six, I used to fold the unwritten portion of my notebooks to make paper airplanes, and when I got older, I had a whole lot of model airplanes hanging from the ceiling of my bedroom. It was because of the guidance and tutelage of David D. Strachan that I was able to become both a military flyer and a professional airline pilot and realize both my dreams. It wasn't until I got to United and saw that I would be training with guys twice my age that I realized what a tremendous amount of information we got from this high school teacher. The reason that is important is because the younger you are when you get hired at an airline, the more seniority you have. And that's when you start to understand how what this guy did, mentoring us through aviation school and college, and us being able to get onto the major airlines to fly the B-727, B-737, B-767/757, B-777, B-747, Airbus-320/319, and B-787 at such a young age, it's powerful."

Andrew Cummings

ANDREW CUMMINGS started at Wingate High School in 1979. Very shortly thereafter he met Mr. Strachan and the rest is history, as they say. "David D. Strachan has been a remarkable human being, a role model, a father figure, not just to myself, but to many of us folks of color who immigrated from the Caribbean, Central America and Canada, or who lived in the New York area. We've continued to communicate with him over the years, directly and indirectly, just about most of our lives."

Andrew graduated from the flight program in 1981 and attended Southeastern Oklahoma State University, where he earned two bachelors' degrees in 1984. Under the direction of Professor Edward Hunnicute in the Aviation Dept., he was allowed to teach an advanced meteorological course while doing graduate work at Southeastern. "It was a very senior-level undergraduate course, mainly tailored to aviation. I taught that class for a semester, and it was wonderful." Andrew completed his master's degree in 1985.

What happened next Andrew describes as "very ritual, a somewhat standardized move-up process." He remained in the Aviation Dept. at Southeastern Oklahoma State University as a flight instructor to build up his flight time and experience, continuing the legacy that began under the tutelage of David D. Strachan at Republic Airport in Farmingdale, L.I., *i.e.*, earning as many Federal

Aviation Administration certificates as one possibly can in a short period of time. Relying on outside resources within the North Texas/Southern Oklahoma area, he completed his multi-engine instructor, multi-engine and single-engine rating with airline transport pilot category, and single and multi-engine ratings. His first non-university position was with Air New Orleans, a small commuter airline connected to Continental Express, from 1986 to 1988. "Again, you're doing everything within your power to gain hours of experience." He transitioned to Conquest Airlines, a regional operator out of Beaumont, TX, that flew to most of the major cities in the region: Houston, San Antonio, Dallas, Austin (the hub), Abilene, Tyler, El Paso, Lubbock, and also New Orleans, Birmingham and points east. After one year at Conquest, he was hired by United Airlines, in September 1989, and has been there just over twenty-five years.

Co-captain of a Boeing 747 jetliner, Andrew is "almost 99%" certain that he would not have been able to achieve any of his successes had he not come into contact with David D. Strachan at Wingate H.S. "Bro. Strachan has always been a very special person, a special teacher. He puts in lots of energy. He's done incredible things and he has tried to be a positive role model for all of us, trying to explain, trying to reinforce, even though he may not have had the same opportunity, and will never achieve the things that he was trying to achieve back in his era, in the fifties and sixties. But us, if we put forth the effort, the energy, and we try to do the best we can, and try to live a clean life, all of the things that he was denied have the possibility of working for us."

Although he was the only "David D. Strachan scholar" at Southeastern Oklahoma State at the time, Andrew kept in touch with his colleagues from Wingate. "I communicated with the guys who went to Alabama Aviation and Technical College and Florida Institute of Technology. Some of our guys also went to the Spartan School of Aeronautics in Tulsa, OK. So I kept in touch, usually by telephone, with most of the guys, or we'd meet up during the holidays back in the Brooklyn." To this day, he keeps in close contact with Anthony Manswell, who arrived at United just 30 days before him in 1989. Their children have grown up together and the two families have enjoyed numerous joint vacations, including ski trips, cruises, and just "hanging out" at each other's homes.

Andrew says that David D. Strachan "always tried to use positive reinforcement to communicate with us all. He never blamed the individual, but the institutionalized racism. He never went back to blame. He doesn't have a chip on his shoulder. He's always spoken to us and communicated to us with clarity. He'd say, 'Forget about him; it's about you. Not what has someone done for you lately, but what can you do for yourself. Let's make this work; let's do what it takes to make this happen. O.K., you're going to run up against a couple of walls, but that's going to happen. Step back. You're not injured; you're not going to die. You just have to move on. You're going to try something else.'"

Andrew hit one of those walls in Dallas, TX, in 1985. "I was there interviewing for a flight instruction position that was being vacated by a gentleman who had graduated from the same university as me and was moving on to a better job. He was the one who told me about it." Andrew submitted his résumé and was called in. The gentleman who conducted the interview, a Brit with a very thick accent, he recalls with clarity, was named Andrew Cumming. He also interviewed two other pilots whom Andrew had told about the job opening. Both had less flight time and fewer academic credentials than Andrew. "When I met with Mr. Cumming, I was taken through an elaborate three-hour interview process that the other two candidates did not experience. Out of nowhere, he started asking me elaborate test questions that he created instantly, just unbelievable stuff for a flight instruction position, books and departure charts and a barrage of questions; it was absolutely incomprehensible. I was not prepared for a test, but I had enough general knowledge in the field that I was actually answering every question. He was rather surprised and at the end he said, 'You know, most guys would have stopped a long time ago. You continued the whole process.' The long and short of the story: I found out a few days later that he hired one of the Caucasian gentlemen I told about the position, someone with *no* experience. Mr. Cumming told me afterward that I came 'very close' and that I should 'hang in there,' that he would give me another shot at it later, but he said that I did not meet the qualifications for what they were looking for."

Andrew says, "It's very, very difficult to obtain the experience you need, and a lot of the companies out there will tell you, 'Oh, you have the certificate. You meet the qualifications.' But at the end of the day, when you show up for a position or get interviewed for the job, they say, 'We'd love to have you here, the process has been wonderful, you meet all the criteria and credentials, but you do not have the experience.' So, experience is very, very important. Today, things are being done a little bit differently. There is something called a special exemption waiver. The entire industry is being waived right now due to the shortage of qualified pilots. Nevertheless, airline companies, whether freight carriers, passenger airlines or private corporations, very often will hire and train white pilots with no experience rather than hire a qualified black pilot with experience."

According to Andrew, David D. Strachan would say, "That's just the facts of life. Now move on."

"For me, personally, he's been a father figure. My father was present, but he was never there in an emotional sense. Bro. Strachan has guided us over the years, trying to give us some sense of direction in our lives. And he has been extraordinarily effective."

Jhonny Polanco

JHONNY POLANCO has been flying with the Alaska Air National Guard since 2006, but earlier in his journey to his present position he encountered many obstacles, including one particular colonel in the Air Force ROTC program at Manhattan College in the Bronx.

"I started attending the College of Aeronautics [now Vaughn College] in 1987 and at the same time I was enrolled in the Air Force ROTC program at Manhattan College because I knew this was one way I could get to be a pilot. After about a year in the program, I approached the detachment commander and said, 'Sir, my desire is to be an officer in the United States Air Force. I know my grades are not the best, but I'm trying really hard and I'm not the dullest tool in the toolbox. I'm kind of in the middle of the pack and I really want to be a pilot.' His reply was, 'I'm sorry, Jhonny. Keep trying, but we don't have any pilot slots for you this year.'"

Jhonny spent the next year improving his military test scores and raising his grades, then tried again. The response was the same, even though several of his classmates were getting pilot slots. "Four or five of them and I said, 'Wow! I need to try harder, that's what I need to do.' Sure enough, I improved my grades and I started taking flying lessons at the airport on Long Island. I spoke with the colonel again and reminded him that I really wanted to be a pilot. His response this time was, 'Well, Jhonny, the best I can offer you is a navigator slot.'" Jhonny protested, "Sir, I've done everything you asked of me and I'm physically fit. I've got everything I need. My scores have improved. I really want to be an Air Force pilot.' And most of the other cadets were getting pilot slots. But he repeated, 'This year I can't offer you a pilot slot' and I was like, wow, this is kind of…weird. What is it that I have failed to do? At the time, I thought it was just that I needed to work harder in my academics and if I did that, it was going to happen."

After being turned down for a pilot slot with the Air Force, Jhonny wrote a letter to the commander removing himself from the Air Force ROTC program. "His answer to me was, 'O.K., fine. Best of luck.'"

Like many young girls and boys, Jhonny Polanco grew up wanting to be an astronaut. "I remember when I was five years old and holding my dad's hand at an air show in the Dominican Republic, watching airplanes do aerobatics, and I remember pulling my dad's hand and telling him, 'I want to do what those guys are doing.'" He believed that the best way to reach his goal was through Air Force pilot training. After moving to the United States with his family in 1979, Jhonny discovered the wonders of free education and public libraries. He was amazed that people could walk into a library, present a library card, and take books home without paying. "So I was taking advantage of all this free education that the U.S. was offering me. It was great, but I still had my dream." It was getting there that presented a problem. Jhonny knew nothing about military service academies when he graduated from Grover Cleveland High School in Queens and later in life he asked both his parents why they hadn't told him about the Air Force Academy: they didn't know it existed.

"I wish I had met David D. Strachan when I was fourteen or fifteen or even younger. I probably would not be in Alaska where I'm living today because my dreams would have been realized a lot younger and I would probably have gone a different route. But I would not be a pilot at all had it not been for Mr. Strachan."

After leaving the ROTC program, out of money and running out of time because of the age limitations placed on pilot training in the military, Jhonny dropped out of college and got a job driving for UPS. "I couldn't afford to take out more student loans and continue paying the ones I had." When he could, Jhonny would practice flying out in Farmingdale. One Sunday afternoon he found himself thinking, "I'm 23, 24 years old with no college degree and no idea how I'm ever going to get back on track to achieve my goal, and I said to my flying instructor, an African American named Sheldon Smith, 'Sheldon, I want to fly for the Air Force. Who do I need to talk to? Who can give me some guidance about that?'"

That was Sunday. The next day, Jhonny visited Wingate High School, which was only a couple of blocks from his UPS route in Brooklyn. "I went over there at lunchtime and asked at the front door to see Mr. Strachan. The school guard sent me upstairs and I sat down with David D. Strachan. I called him 'Sir' and I told him what it was I wanted to do." Because it was the middle of the school day, David D. Strachan arranged for them to meet at his home the following evening. The first thing he did was set Jhonny Polanco straight on what had happened to him in the ROTC program. "He broke it down. He said, 'These are the requirements that you need to be an astronaut. These are the requirements that you need to be an Air Force pilot,' and I told him, 'Well, Sir, I've done this and I've done that and you know, I think I've done everything I could in my power, except earn my degree.' He said, 'I bet most of the other kids that were getting the pilot slots were Caucasian,' and I was like, 'Yeah, how did you know?' So then he said, 'Well, let me tell you a story,' and he pretty much opened my eyes to what was going on. It didn't matter how hard I was trying, if I didn't have the proper 'credential' that was needed, I wasn't going to make it anywhere. And he told me, 'This is where you are today, these are the steps that you need to take. Finish that degree and once we get through that step, then we'll go to the next step.' He pretty much drew me a roadmap, if you will, of what I needed to accomplish to get to where I wanted to be.

"The biggest challenge for me was getting my degree. Once that was done, it was just a matter of applying to the Air National Guard. It was like starting all over again because a lot of universities would not accept all of my credits from previous studies. I was also still working for UPS and going to school part-time." Jhonny was finally able to obtain a B.S. degree from the City University of Bellevue, Washington in 1996, but by then, he was already aged-out of the flight training programs for the Air Force and the Navy. He joined the Marine Corps in 1997 under an age waiver program for Hispanics. He completed their flight program, earned his pilot wings, and flew for the Marine Corps for nine and a half years.

Jhonny considers himself one of the lucky ones, having met David D. Strachan while he was still young enough to achieve his goal of becoming a pilot. "I am so lucky to have met him when I did. By the time you get to college, you're already behind, and that's a shame. When I got hired to the Air National Guard, I was a senior captain in the Marine Corps, but they were like, 'Well, the Marine Corps is not part of the Guard.' If I had joined the Guard from the very beginning, I would have been growing in the Guard and I would probably have been further along in my career. I'm still struggling with that."

Jhonny had applied to Air National Guard units in several states, including New York, Mississippi and Arizona, as well as Puerto Rico. Alaska was the only state that responded to his résumé, so he joined the 168th Air Refueling Wing in Alaska where he is currently serving. Had he never met David D. Strachan, Jhonny Polanco says he thinks he would still be delivering boxes for UPS in New York. "Nothing wrong with that, it's just that my dream, my aspirations would have never been realized.

"Bro. Strachan was the compass in my life that got me to where I needed to be. He was that lighthouse that showed me the way.

Every time I had an issue or came across something weird, I'd send him an email and ask, 'Hey, Bro. Strachan, what do you think about this?' and he'd reply, 'Well, Jhonny, this is what you can do,' and sure enough, they were all right things. He's so instrumental. I can't thank him enough. I owe him a lot."

Now, when David D. Strachan asks a favor of Jhonny, he doesn't hesitate. "One time he told me, 'I need you to go talk to this kid in Alabama about Aviation Technical College,' where he used to send most of his students. A week later I was there talking to that person." Jhonny is a member of OBAP (the Organization of Black Aeronautics Professionals) and works actively with them to recruit black and Latino pilots into the Air National Guard. He also keeps in touch with his colleagues who have traveled the pipeline into the commercial aviation industry to try to get black and Latino men and women into pilot positions there.

"I think the network that Bro. Strachan created with all of us, we need to continue that and it doesn't have to be just minorities. There are some young white kids that are struggling out there. Let's bring them on board and show them the way, too. Maybe these individuals, whenever they move up the ladder, will say, 'Hey, you know what? It was somebody from a different race that helped me get in here.' Maybe we'll start changing their minds and changing the culture so that two, three hundred years from now, it'll be the same for everybody. At least that's my dream, that's my hope."

Even now, as an O-4 [major] about to be promoted to O-5 [lieutenant colonel] in military rank, Jhonny feels that he and others like him are not being groomed for senior positions in the Air National Guard. "Maybe it's because I didn't grow up here [in the U.S.] or maybe they're just keeping it a secret or something. I don't know what the case may be, but it goes back to what Bro. Strachan told me years ago: [discrimination] is no longer done in your face. It's now done behind closed doors, by not grooming you or not sending you to the schools required for future success. It's done by not giving you the opportunities that you need to excel. It's like a velvet knife, if you will. However, my drive is still there. I wasn't the first to go through the headaches and I will not be the last. There are still people out there who have malice in their minds.

"I once asked him, 'Bro. Strachan, why do you do this?' I spent a lot of time at his home in Brooklyn and he actually told me, 'Jhonny, I get a sense of happiness when I see kids like you wearing the uniform, flying in the military, working in the airlines. I get a sense of, I guess, pride and joy.' That's what he told me, it brings him joy. I said, 'You know, Bro. Strachan, I never thought about it that way, but I could see how that could be a big thing in life.' I can just imagine the feeling that comes to him when I send him pictures of me with a note, 'Hey, Bro. Strachan, this is where I am right now,' knowing that he gets joy out of that. Had it not been for him, none of us would have been where we are. We'd probably be struggling, still…."

Jason Matthews

My name is JASON MATTHEWS and I am a former student of Bro. Strachan (1988-1991). In the group photo, I'm the one standing directly behind his right shoulder wearing a black jacket with white shirt.

Ever since I was a kid I wanted to be a pilot, but I had no idea how, where, etc. Wingate High School was *not* my first choice. In fact, it wasn't a choice at all. Truth be told, my grades weren't good enough to get into the high schools of my choice. Wingate was my zoned school and that's where I ended up.

My first day and every day thereafter in Bro. Strachan's class was a life's lesson. He made sure we were prepared for the outside world in every way: in the way we spoke, the way we dressed, the way we carried ourselves, and in our goals and expectations. We weren't going to finish school to become janitors (with all due respect to janitors). He made us believe that pilots weren't just old white men who we saw on television or walking through JFK airport. According to Bro. Strachan, we could become pilots, doctors, lawyers—anything we wanted, but mainly, those of us who took his classes wanted to be pilots. His impact was so obvious that other teachers and students could recognize those of us who were his students. I wasn't a troubled kid, but I would've been one of those adults who never rose to his full potential had it not been for Bro. Strachan. He was a great academic teacher, but his most important impact came from his conversations and advice on life and African/Negro history.

Bro. Strachan's word carries a lot of respect. If he's involved in a matter, that issue will get the attention it deserves.

I've never personally or professionally encountered discriminatory behavior myself, even though I went to flight school in Alabama in a predominantly white environment. We had a close-knit group that stuck together and we were in constant communication with Bro. Strachan. Being a former student and friend of his is equivalent to being a member of a secret society, and although I haven't myself been in a position to help others, once you've been through "the system" with Bro. Strachan, helping one another would be the natural thing to do.

I was very instrumental in planning the reunion that took place on 23 October 2010, arranging the time, ordering food, etc. Once I notified everyone of the event, getting folks to show up was the easy part. Anything involving the Brother becomes priority. All together, there were about 35-40 people in attendance. By the time the group photo was taken, quite a few people had already left. There was also a video made of folks telling their stories during the reunion. The reunion was a great success; folks attended from all over the country and some who were working overseas attended, also.

Being a pilot was the only thing I ever wanted to do, and although I took the "scenic route" to getting there, I've never allowed that fire to die. No one could've deterred me, not family, friends, nor financial issues. In March 2015, I began flying as a junior pilot with an aerial surveying/photography company, Control Cam. My advice to others who would like to pursue this path is simply a repeat of what I've learned from Bro. Strachan: Never give up!

Jason Matthews

Leaford Daley

LEAFORD DALEY flies for Alpha Star Aviation Services in Riyadh, Saudi Arabia, where he is the captain of a Gulfstream-550 serving primarily the Ministry of the Interior of that country. He attended George Wingate High School in Brooklyn, New York, from 1987 to 1990.

"When I went to junior high school, [I] asked which school you're supposed to apply to for aviation, so I applied to a school called Park West. They turned me down. They were sending me to my zoned school and it was the same school my sister was going to. Well, all my other Jamaican friends were going to Wingate, so I decided, 'I'm not going to school [with] my sister. I'll go where my friends [are going].' I showed up at the school with everybody and they were like, 'Why are you here?' I said, 'I don't know, they must have mixed up my records.' And the school people took me in without checking my records or verifying that I'm supposed to be in that school. That's how I ended up at Wingate. I didn't know the school had an aviation program. I just accidentally went there. The first day there the counselor said to me, 'What are you interested in?' I said, 'I'm interested in aviation' and she said, 'Oh, we have an aviation program here.' I was like, *Really?* And she said, 'You want me to sign you up for it?' That's how I ended up being put into the class.

"The first time I met [David D. Strachan], he didn't come off as being the teacher I was expecting to change my life. He had a strong grip on the students and he knew who were the idlers and who were the serious ones, and so he would group everybody in that same [group] until you proved otherwise. I remember a few times when we were supposed to go out to the airport [for] flight experience, and he said, 'Be here at 7 a.m.' Once I showed up at 7:05 and he said, 'Oh, welcome!' and then he *shut* the bus door in my face and drove off! He did that to me, I swear. I was really angry, you know, but it taught me a lesson, to be on time.

"Some of the other students in the class, whenever he was talking about life and what he's seeing taking place in America, a lot of the guys from the islands would say, 'Oh, Mr. Strachan is a racist guy. He doesn't understand.' He [would] always ask the class, 'What is the population of the student body in this school?' And the population was mostly from the Caribbean and black Americans, and probably five percent was from Puerto Rico or Santo Domingo or some other Spanish-speaking country. And he always said, 'You have a student body [that is] 95 percent African descent and teachers in the school, less than ten percent are from African descent and 90 percent of the teachers are white.' So he always used to say, 'Do you think these teachers here are going to make you compete with their sons and daughters in this world that you're now going into? I mean, do you think they really are here to make sure you're going to compete with their children?' That always stood out in my mind when he said that.

"I believed him because, in every class I went to, every time I wanted to go flying, these teachers would never sign the paperwork to let me go [to the airport]. They would always say, 'Oh, you shouldn't be doing that; that's a waste of time. You should do something else.' And I always remember that." When several of his teachers refused to sign his paperwork, despite his passing grades and his high motivation, Leaford had to devise his own method of getting around the white-supremacy racism that is endemic to the

New York City school system. "After a while, I didn't tell Bro. Strachan what I was doing because I already made up my mind, once I get them to sign it, I make a copy of it and every time [after that], I just scribbled their signature. I'm sorry I had to do that, but flying was what I wanted to do. I would make up their class session, but they just did not want to sign the paper for me to go flying.

"Something I learned later on, and I tell other people now, is this: I think growing up in the Caribbean, compared to growing up in the U.S., [helps] create the person you're going to be in life. It helps you develop worth. Growing up in the islands, when you go to hospitals, what you see is mostly African-looking doctors and nurses. When I was growing up in Jamaica, we had only one T.V. station, but the actors, the reporters in the field, they all looked like me. When you went to the airport, the pilots also looked like me. So it created an image in your head that there's nothing you cannot do because there's someone like you already doing it. But when you come to America, you do not see that. And I think that has an effect on young Africans and African Americans in the community, because they do not see that, and if they don't see it, they don't think they can achieve it."

After graduating from Wingate, Leaford became an avid follower of David D. Strachan. "Bro. Strachan was funneling all of us to Alabama Aviation and Technical College (AATC), where you got all your pilot licenses and your ratings. At the same time, I was going to Enterprise Junior College down the road because AATC was a vocational school, so it didn't [offer] all the requirements for a two-year degree." After graduation, he stayed on in Alabama to see if he could get a job as a flight instructor, but that didn't work out, so he came home. "I wanted to come back to New York to help the guys from the high school that I went to into the same program. The college I wanted to go to was very expensive, and I didn't want to break my mother because she had already spent a lot of money for me to go to Alabama." So Leaford attended York College in Queens, but he did not graduate. "I took a lot of classes, but I never finished. And I've never acquired my four-year degree." So from 1994 until 1998, Leaford was doing odd jobs and keeping his certified flight instructor (CFI) license. "I joined a civil air patrol, which patrolled for small airplanes that crashed. I also mentored in a military auxiliary program to keep kids that were in high school interested in flying.

"It was actually Bro. Strachan who got me my first job flying. I went to those companies that had U.S. government contracts, but they kept turning me down. I stayed in New York over a two-year period trying to get on with them. Finally, Bro. Strachan had had enough and he told the company he was going to pull the contract if they did not hire some [of us]. And, of course, they told Bro. Strachan, 'We don't know any black pilots.' So Bro. Strachan told a few of us to bring our résumés and he asked me if I knew anyone else, and I knew other people I've met over the years. I pulled, I think, maybe 25 résumés together and gave the package to him. He walked into their office and dropped the résumés and they ended up hiring about ten of us. And I was able to affect the next generation that was coming behind me." Both of those companies that had government contracts on Long Island, Nassau Fliers and Flight Ways, are no longer in business.

In 2000, Leaford got a job flying bank checks at night from Buffalo, New York to the Federal Reserve Bank in Cleveland, Ohio. In 2002, he was hired by Mesa Airlines, a feeder company for several major airlines including United, U.S. Air and Delta. "For two years, I flew a Brazilian-made plane out of Washington, D.C., as a first officer, and another two years as the captain." Then, roughly in October of 2006, he went to Kuwait. "That was my first job overseas, flying the same plane, the EMB-145. The company in Kuwait had the airplane decked out as a corporate jet, not as a passenger plane. I flew with them into 2007, and I started networking and meeting other pilots. One of them told me about his company, Net Jet Middle East, which is based in Jeddah, Saudi Arabia, and said they were looking for pilots. So I applied and got the job. I was there from 2007 until 2012 flying an American-built plane, the Gulfstream-450." In 2012, Leaford moved over to his current position with Alpha Star where he flies the larger Gulfstream-550. "The same license is required for both airplanes, but the first one carries twelve passengers and this one carries sixteen."

Leaford tells a personal story about how funny life is. "If I had the foresight, maybe I would have been [in Saudi Arabia] from when I left college. When the first Gulf War was taking place, we were always glued to the T.V. when we had a break from class. Well, I was watching what they called the Desert Shield, and then the Desert Storm. There were three Saudi guys that were in school with us and I remember when one of them was leaving, he said to me, 'You could come to Saudi, man. I can get you a job at this airline in Saudi, trust me.' I [thought], 'What in the world is this guy talking about?' I had not a clue where that part of the world was!"

Though seemingly smooth, Leaford's progression from Wingate H.S. to captain of a Gulfstream-550 was not without incident. He says about his experience of *washing out*, "This is something I would say has happened to all of us. When you get hired at an airline, you go through the interview process. Someone in the interview takes a liking to your abilities and they hire you. But then you have to go through the training process, which is separate [from] human resources. The people in the training department are the ones who decide how [many] of us they're going to let into the company."

That training process, according to Leaford, takes place in three stages. First, there is a month of ground training where you learn the system on the particular aircraft you'll be operating. Then you go into a simulator to practice emergency landings and other procedures. In stage three, you actually train with passengers aboard an airplane, flying as the first officer under the direction of a captain. "When we go to the simulator," says Leaford, "that is the point where a majority of us get washed out. You have Caucasians that you have to get past in order to get to the stage of actually flying passengers. It's a common problem for us; almost anyone of us you talk to will tell you, 'I went to this place and I washed out.'" Leaford washed out at American Eagle, the regional flyer for American Airlines.

"That's the first time *it* hit me, but when I went to Mesa, and met others like me, I found out there were four or five of us who went to American Eagle over the years and we were all washed out. You'll find that there are so many stories of brothers who went through the same thing. You go to an airline and you think you're finally getting someplace and then [you're] pushed back out the door. You tell your friends, you tell your family, and then, you know, it's devastating when they get rid of you."

But Leaford says that the most important lesson he learned from David D. Strachan concerned not aviation, but how to navigate his way around this devastation. "Bro. Strachan used to say, 'I am not here to teach you how to fly. That is not my job. What I am here to do is teach you how to deal with the people you will have to deal with in your future.' He used the term 'landmine.' He would say, 'They are going to put so [many] landmines in your way. I'm here to show you how to tippy-toe around the landmines.'

"I see a lot of us fall off to the wayside or give up because they never fully understood what Bro. Strachan was trying to instill in them. Some people thought what he was saying was incorrect and then when these landmines, these roadblocks, got in their way, they didn't know how to deal with it. I've come across so [many] pilots over the years that I thought were really good pilots, really *great* pilots, but they could not navigate the roadblocks and a lot of them just gave up and walked away. I thought it was a big loss. Some of them were friends of mine and I'm kind of angry sometimes because I said, 'This guy has the potential to go further in his life,' but he couldn't handle it because he never listened to what Bro. Strachan was telling us. And the ones who are still in aviation and still fighting are the ones who worked hard and took the lesson.

"Everywhere I go, I try to make connections and once a job

comes available, I kind of find people work or call people and say, 'Hey, this company's hiring. I have a friend over there. He's willing to take you on.' Right now, I'm building a network of guys out there to try to get as [many] people as we can into anywhere I can find, and try to create a way to keep guys employed. That's what I've been doing for the last eight years since I've been over here."

In the tradition of David D. Strachan, Leaford teaches young people to recognize the fact that there is nothing wrong with them when the system slaps them in the face and tells them 'no.' "I learned from another pilot that anything in America that pays [well]—doesn't matter if you're a doctor, a lawyer, a pilot—once the money starts going over a hundred thousand, they will fight you tooth and nail for it. That is the key to what they're doing and they're going to try to put every roadblock in your way because they don't want you to make that type of salary. They want you to make the lower-end salary which is not a threat to them."

His advice to aspiring pilots whenever they encounter roadblocks and landmines is to talk to somebody else who has been through it and ask, *How did you handle it?* "If you shut down, then you'll never get anywhere because you'll always go hide when things go wrong and you cannot do that. That's one of the biggest things you have to try to teach younger people, not to shut down, because if you shut down, that means they've won!"

Willis Reid

WILLIS REID met David D. Strachan at Wingate High School when he was already in the flight program. "We had a couple of other teachers before him and it was halfway through my junior year, getting into my senior year, when he came to Wingate. Here was this teacher who seemed like he was really into getting us to do what we were supposed to do, which was study and get the work done. It was good to see [a black teacher], for sure, but the question was, *O.K., what's he going to teach us?* He made sure that he got people in line. Since I was interested in learning, it didn't bother me. There were a few guys in the program who were there because they could be there. But there were also guys like me who were really motivated to learn to fly. So when he came into the program, he didn't take any mess from these youngsters. I mean, he was fair, but he was an *O.K., let's get it done* sort of person." Willis remembers that he was the first student to solo in high school under the tutelage of David D. Strachan, followed by Hilbert Smith and then, one by one, a few of the other students.

"He's an incredible person. In the many years I've known him, he's helped so many people." Willis, who left home at eighteen and has been on his own ever since, says that he used to receive motivational letters from David D. Strachan. "He always sent me a letter [that said], 'You can do it!' And he's been known to give guys money over the years. A friend of mine, one of the guys I'm really close to, said that when he was broke, he got this letter in the mail, something to the effect of 'Enjoy yourself,' with a money order in it."

After graduating from high school, Willis attended the Spartan School of Aeronautics in Tulsa, Oklahoma, one of two from his Wingate class to venture out West for training. But he didn't go there to fly; he went to get his airframe and power plant (A&P) certification to become a technician. After graduating from Spartan, he paid his way through the Florida Institute of Technology by working as an aircraft mechanic. He remembers an incident that happened at Wingate. "I walked into the class, and I don't remember this guy's last name, but his first name was Chris—I always remember because he lived not too far from me—and Mr. Strachan was talking to him and telling him what he should do when he graduated. Well, Chris said to him, 'I don't know what to do. I want to be a pilot. I want to be an aircraft mechanic,' and Mr. Strachan said to him, 'Why don't you do both?' I was putting my books in the desk, getting ready to sit down, and I'm standing there, listening to this conversation because my seat was right in front of Chris' and I thought, *That's it! This man is CRAZY. How the heck can you do both?* You know, when you're young, you don't know these things. I listened to a lot of things Mr. Strachan had to say. I always believed what he told us, but this was too much. And guess what? I went on to get my A&P to work on aircraft, and also my pilot's license. I reminded him of it some years later, but when you're seventeen, you just don't think it's possible.

"I think it was wisdom, age and the fact that [David D. Strachan] thought that we could do anything we put our minds to. He wanted us to believe in ourselves. We've seen it many times. These guys are out there *doing it*, like he used to tell us. But he said something else that was very important. He said, 'You're going to be up against people with a lot more experience, youngsters your age who have many hours already, way more than you do. You know why? Because they grew up on a big farm and they had an airplane that they learned to take off and land. They fly because they're so far away from anybody that they have to, just to visit their neighbors and go into town. They have crop-dusters and they're flying airplanes from the day they were born.' I realized it later on when I went to college and guys [would say], 'My daddy has a Cessna,' and I'm thinking, 'Bro. Strachan told us that when we were in high school.' I'll always remember that."

Willis comes from a "typical" West Indian family of African, British, Indian and Chinese ancestry. He moved to the United States when he was ten or eleven years old. He got interested in flying in junior high school by putting together model planes, particularly WWII fighters, but even before that, when he was living with his grandparents in the Jamaican countryside, he was fascinated by a crop-duster that would fly over in the mornings. "The guy in the airplane would wave to us and I always thought that was pretty cool." One morning, as it was flying directly overhead, Willis heard a big bang and the airplane went completely quiet. "I looked up and thought, 'Ah, I never heard that before.'" The pilot ended up crash-landing in a nearby field. "He didn't pick the best spot, but he survived." Willis didn't meet the pilot, but he was fascinated by the airplane. "It kind of stuck in the back of my mind." Years later, in New York, when it was time to pick a high school, he chose Aviation High School in Queens where he could earn either an airframe or a power plant certification before graduating, but he couldn't get there to take the exam. "So I ended up going to Wingate instead, a few blocks from my house. It worked out great."

Willis recalls fondly that, even in high school, David D. Strachan encouraged his students to eat healthily. "He's always wanted us to be vegetarians, for years. And then one day I decided, *You know what?* I want to stop eating meat, which I grew up on. I'm going to stop eating steak and see what happens. That was probably twenty years ago. I didn't miss it. I have to keep tabs on [my cholesterol] I discovered a few years ago, so if I had continued eating that stuff all those years, who knows what would have happened? It takes so long to digest that stuff, you know."

It was David D. Strachan who recommended the Spartan School of Aeronautics to Willis. "He had all these things all lined up for us. I just told that to one of the pilots I flew with today because his son is learning how to fly. I said, 'One thing you have to do, you have to stay in the South. Bro. Strachan told us that, years ago. You don't fly because you waste so many hours [in northern schools]. You learn something today, the weather gets bad for a week, then you have to re-learn it a week later, unless you're really, really sharp. You do a lot of 'desk flying' in the North, I mean, they didn't have computers and all that stuff when I was younger."

A couple of years after graduating from the Florida Institute of Technology, Willis landed his dream job of flying the Gulfstream Four (G-4), which he had also worked on as an A&P mechanic. He flew the G-4 for just under six years and then, in 1997, was hired by Northwest Airlines where he was type-rated on the Boeing 747-400 and the Airbus 330. In 2009, Northwest merged with Delta Airlines and he now flies as first officer (co-pilot) on the Airbus 330.

Although Willis has never been involved in any litigation against any airline to obtain a job, he is fully cognizant of the fact that he has his position because of others who have gone before him. "I firmly believe that if they didn't have the lawsuits and certain things weren't put in place, it's highly probable that I wouldn't be flying for a major U.S. airline. I'd probably be overseas right now. I wouldn't be flying for an airline here in the States. And that's one of the things I say everyday. When I go to work and have a bad day with somebody, I say, *You know what?* I've got it pretty easy because the Tuskegee Airmen never even got a chance. Bro. Strachan never got a chance. So I know, no matter how bad it is, it's still easier than what they went through."

For three decades, Willis and his wife have been sponsoring a young person somewhere in the world who is growing up without the advantages they have had. "Right now, it's two: one in Africa and one in South America. I've made it a point because we're not here in this world for ourselves. That's what life is about. There are so many people so much smarter than me who just don't have that opportunity, and that's unfortunate."

Diane Pencil

My name is DIANE ANGELA PENCIL and I currently work for Arik Air as a pilot in Lagos, Nigeria. I attended George W. Wingate High School from September 1984 through January 1988. I stumbled across the aviation program during the recruitment of a friend by her guidance counselor. I begged him to enroll me into the program, also. In September 1985, my life changed for the better. I was a shy, petite fifteen-year-old with very little self-confidence. I had recently immigrated from Birmingham, England, and was having a hard time "fitting in" amongst my peers.

Bro. Strachan, as we fondly referred to him, had an attendance book with our names written in it. I remember him calling us up to his desk one-by-one, where we were asked to confirm the spelling of our names. "Speak up, sister." We were also asked what we wanted to become once we finished college. I told Bro. Strachan that I wanted to be a flight attendant. I remember his response: "Okay sister, why not a pilot?" He had a big smile on his face. I responded that I didn't know girls could be pilots. He crossed out "stewardess" in his attendance book and wrote "pilot," then smiled at me again.

Over the decades there have been many uphill battles, yet Bro. Strachan remained relentless in his efforts to encourage me to continue moving forward. He has been a teacher, a father, a mentor, a lifeline, and most importantly, he showed me unconditional love. I could not have made this journey without him. I am a certified flight instructor. I have also taught simulator training and I worked for several commuter airlines while living in the United States. I currently hold six type ratings. My last six years have been spent flying over West Africa, along with line training pilots on a regional jet. I am currently captain of a Boeing 737-NG.

I continuously thank God for placing Bro. Strachan, and all my aviation brothers and sisters, in my life.

Diane Pencil

Ian Abraham

I am IAN ABRAHAM and I first met Mr. Strachan as a student at Boys and Girls High School in Brooklyn. I was always interested in aviation and I chose the class because I wanted to become an airline pilot. There were three high schools that offered aviation programs, but I was unable to get in and as an alternative, I attended Boys and Girls, which fortunately had an aviation program, also. When I met Mr. Strachan, he was a breath of fresh air and I was totally impressed with his enthusiasm, his teaching methods, and his demeanor.

Not only did Mr. Strachan speak eloquently about aviation, but also about life, business and things in general. While in class, I found myself looking forward to attending his next class. Not only was he an aviation instructor, his classes were like being in a social studies class or a current events class because of the fact that he dealt with so many subjects. He often referred to each student as a scholar, just to remind us that we all had great potential to excel in whatever endeavor we may pursue. Additionally, he showed total respect for each student and we reciprocated accordingly. Based on his character and his teaching methodology, which exemplified excellence, he also commanded respect from us. We could not help but respect him. He led by example. Whenever anyone left his class, one felt fulfilled and that one had the ability to accomplish anything he or she wanted.

Throughout the many years in which I have known Mr. Strachan, his advice has always been impeccable; he is a man who does not believe that anything is impossible and the word "cannot" is not a part of his vocabulary.

After my one semester with Mr. Strachan, his departure left many students disappointed and we knew that a great void could not be filled. Happily, he transferred to Wingate High School, where he was able to help and influence a greater number of students. Even to this day, he continues to influence myself and the pilots who are well into their profession, and I believe that, although he has officially retired, he will never retire from helping others.

Based upon the many career-oriented student who graduated under Mr. Strachan's leadership, one can conclude that he had a great influence on all of his students and the many people he encountered. I have the utmost respect for Mr. Strachan and I think he is one of the finest human beings that I ever came across. Whether one pursued an aviation career or chose another profession, his patience, persistence and diligent attitude helped everyone who crossed his path. Words alone cannot convey what this man has done and I am honored to have shared this space on Earth with him. I am a complete man as a result of his teaching.

Ian Abraham

Tracey Gray

A 1986 graduate of Tilden High School in Brooklyn, TRACEY GRAY found out about David D. Strachan through an elementary school friend, Disdale Enton, who went to Wingate High School. "I knew about the program at Wingate, but I just didn't want to go there," he confesses. "I didn't know how great the program was. [Disdale] was always telling me what he was doing, and when it was time to go to college, he told me he was going to Alabama. I was thinking maybe he was going to Tuskegee, but no, he went *further* down south to Alabama Aviation and Technical College (AATC) to get his ratings. I wanted to stay here and fly at Republic Airport in Farmingdale. I gave up on that because I saw they had no intention of getting me where I wanted to go. And that's when I went down to Alabama."

David D. Strachan has been instrumental to Tracey's career from the inception. "I used to come here [David D. Strachan's living room] and do my written exams. And then he would talk to us, just a little conversation, and tell us what we needed to do. We all wanted to do it, but even wanting, you still have no direction. He was like the only one that gave us that direction." Tracey tells everybody he meets that the Strachan residence was the 'mill factory' in Brooklyn out of which they all grew. "Everybody at Wingate came out of here, or he touched someone's hands. Even out of

August Martin High School, he helped those students. And Park West High School, he cranked them out. Nobody even knew about the opportunities that we had. There was no guidance [from the school system] because they kept us in positions that they felt we should or could achieve. Their whole outlook was that this wasn't something for you. They didn't know our potential. They didn't care. If I was bouncing a basketball or catching a football, that's all well and good, but to actually use my brain? Maybe they didn't think I had a brain."

In Tracey's experience, the private flight schools in many cases "were not receptive for us to fly or to have opportunities. The attitude was often, 'You don't belong here.' You had to do your own due diligence and that is how I found out about AATC, through other students. Some of the instructors had no interest in actually teaching you. They were just looking to make money. You go up for an hour and it's a wasted hour because the instructor gets his flight time off your dollar. Whether you learn anything or not, he's still going to log that time into his logbook." Tracey says there were occasions when the flight instructor never let him touch the controls.

"And I could say, even in Alabama, if it wasn't for [Anthony] Manswell, Richard John, Kendrick Antoine and Neville Giles, if it wasn't for *them* being there, who knows what would have happened to us—Leroy Kinlocke, O'Neil Barnes and myself—because they kind of took us under their wing and got us through the program. Those four got their instructor's rating and stayed and helped everybody else." Tracey was able to earn his flight instructor rating also, but he didn't stay at AATC because of his desire to join the military.

After graduating, Tracey attended St. Francis College in Brooklyn where he earned a bachelor's degree in business administration and airway science in 1989. He then got his master's degree in civil engineering from Brooklyn Polytechnic Institute in 1991. From 1995 to 2003, he served in the D.C. Air National Guard, flying missions on C22B and C21 planes out of Andrews AFB.

"Every Memorial Day weekend, we used to fly down to Maxwell AFB for the Tuskegee Airmen fly-in. One year we went down there, I think it was in 1998 or 1999, and we had probably every [kind of aircraft] in the military inventory, from Cobra helicopters to F-16s, F-15s, and A-10s. When our guys would pull into the parking spots, we would laugh because the ground crews, white guys who were probably in their late forties or early fifties, had probably never seen so many black guys when they dropped their masks, popping out of the airplanes. They were like, *'They're colored flyers!'* They didn't know what to do with themselves! I mean, we had from lieutenants up to colonels, all black aviators. I was a first lieutenant at the time, or maybe a captain. Tony [Manswell] was a captain. Every sort of [aircraft], from fighters to tankers to helicopters, was on the ramp and it was black people flying them. That was the best part. Then the students came out on Saturday. I think it helped for them to see something that they could achieve, not that negative 'pull-back' that you always get."

Tracey admits that he experiences 'pull-back' occasionally and when that happens, he contacts someone who has gone before him. "Trust me, if I'm feeling it now, they must have felt it earlier. How did they deal with it? And that's the way it's been from Day One. If I'm getting the punishment now, they've already had it. And I have never experienced someone not helping me. They will always say, 'Hey, try this. This is how I dealt with it.' I have never gotten a negative response from anybody."

Captain on the Airbus 321, Tracey has been flying for American Airlines for seventeen years. Prior to that, he flew the Boeing 767 and before that, the Airbus 300, making mostly transcontinental flights from New York to Los Angeles and San Francisco. His next goal, he says, probably a year or two down the line, is to become an Airbus instructor, but he adds, "We'll see how it works out," noting that black pilots at American "are like the vanilla beans in Breyer's® ice cream."

Tracey's advice to young people is, "You don't have to bounce a ball; you can do something else. It's a decent profession, but you're not cornered into just being an athlete or entertainer. You have a brain. You can use it. It's great to see people in the STEM disciplines [science, technology, engineering and mathematics], to know that you can go to school and be an engineer. You can go to school and study science."

Wayne Brown

WAYNE BROWN graduated from Wingate High School in 1991. "The great thing about Bro. Strachan, as we call him, is that he's been an all-in-one package for most of us. Wingate H.S. at the time wasn't known to be one of the best high schools in New York City. It was a zoned school, so typically what happens with zoned schools is that you have students who didn't get accepted to other schools end up, by default, going to Wingate from junior high schools in the area. But I got accepted to a couple of other schools, including Aviation High, August Martin and Park West. These were all schools that had [aviation] programs as well. It was through laziness that I went to Wingate, and it worked out to be one of the best non-decisions I ever made because I didn't want to get up early in the morning to go to Queens or Manhattan. I didn't want to do the train. And I had a lot of cousins that went to Wingate, so it was a blessing in disguise."

Wayne was eleven years old when his family came to the United States. Typical of other Caribbean families, he says his parents did not know how to navigate the system when they first arrived. "Having Mr. Strachan there allowed us to gain greater insight as to how to get from Point A to Point B to become a pilot. Mr. Strachan was like a mentor. He was a teacher, but he was a pupil at times, I'm sure. And I think also a father figure to some." Wayne says that he will never forget that this "very charismatic" person wrote his phone number on the board the very first day of class and said, 'Any time you need to call me, here's my number.' "I still remember the number and it hasn't changed since I was in high school, and he probably had it before that." He also describes David D. Strachan as a cheerleader. "He cheered you on when you were doing well and he also disciplined or chastised you when necessary. One of the things he didn't do, he didn't really sugarcoat stuff, as you can tell. He's very direct about most things, gentle, kind, caring, but direct. Those are just some of the things that come to mind when I think of Mr. Strachan."

Wayne is currently first officer on the Boeing 757 and 767 at United Airlines. He began at Continental in March 2007 and has been with United since the two companies merged. He believes that one of the greatest legacies he has acquired from David D. Strachan is the practice of mentoring. The day he arrived in Ozark, Alabama to attend Alabama Aviation and Technical College (AATC) with his mother, Leroy Kinlocke, another Wingate graduate, took them in. "We were going to stay at a hotel, but he was like, 'Nope, you guys stay right here at my apartment.' He just welcomed us in. I was already part of the family and that put my mother at ease knowing that she was leaving her son in Alabama in good hands. I look back at it now and I realize that she probably had some reservations about the whole situation.

"And guys that came after me, I was in a position to mentor them as their flight instructor. One of those guys, Vaslav Patterson, is a pilot at United Airlines. He's ahead of me right now in terms of when he got hired, but I soloed Vas at AATC when I was a flight instructor there."

After graduating from Wingate H.S., Wayne attended Medgar Evers College in Brooklyn for a while. "I didn't really decide what I was going to do as far as the aviation program until later, and I think I missed the boat." He started at AATC a year later and finished the program in two years, followed by a year of flight instructing. After earning a B.S. in business administration at Troy State University in 1997, he returned to New York to work in accounting for a few months while trying to figure out what to do next. That's when being a member of a mutually-supportive "circle of friends" kicked in. "A friend who was flight instructing in New Jersey called and said, 'Hey, Wayne, we need people, get over here.' So I accepted a job flight instructing out at Teeterboro Airport.

"I sent out résumés to regional airlines while I was flight instructing. I was hired by a freight company based in Bennington, Vermont, but they had locations in Columbus, Ohio and Knoxville, Tennessee, so I chose Columbus. I was flying-on-demand, living on a pager, delivering car parts, mainly. It was definitely some interesting flying, all over the country, but living on a pager is tough. You could not be alerted for the whole day and then at 3:00 a.m., you get that call to go somewhere." Wayne was with the freight company for seven months, building his flight time. In 2000, with the encouragement of Anthony Manswell, another Wingate student and mentor, he went through the rigorous selection process for the 109th Airlift Wing of the New York Air National Guard, eventually transferring to the 105th Airlift Wing where he still serves.

His military experience in specialized undergraduate pilot training was not that different from David D. Strachan's in the 1950s. "A lot of these guys that you're in class with, they've somehow, whether it's through college, ROTC, the Air Force Academy, wherever, they have crossed paths and are more aware of the demands of training. In the Guard, you're coming in as somebody that likely will not know anyone, so initially you have to stand alone. One of the things that Bro. Strachan had to learn the hard way, unfortunately, is that you have to go there prepared. You're thinking that it's going to be an environment where they teach you: they do, but they don't." Wayne says that one of his sources of motivation has always been the fact that the Tuskegee Airmen, highly decorated black officers who fought in WWII, came back to the U.S. after the war and couldn't get flying jobs.

Summing up his life's experience since meeting David D. Strachan, Wayne reminisces, "I don't think we realized until now how important this was. It kept us out of trouble. It kept us focused. It kept us motivating each other. For example, when Charles Tai came down [to Alabama] and he's [zooming] through the program, everybody was like, 'Wait a minute: I need to be hustling up, too. I'm wasting time!' So you get that second fire, that 'Hey, I need to start getting on the schedule more.' Tony's another one, Anthony Manswell. He's definitely a fast burner. He finished that program in no time.

"Time is very important to Mr. Strachan and even now, it's so important because you take what I'm doing now. That probably comes from his military background, but he passed that down to us. For example, we used to go out to Republic Airport once a week to do our flight training and the bus would leave at a specific time. One of the things that really stood out in watching other people was when Mr. Strachan said we were leaving at 7:15. It was not 7:16. It was not 7:14. So it kind of makes you want it, and if you really want it, you're going to be there with enough time to get on the bus to leave at 7:15. I remember instances where people showed up at 7:16 thinking they would get on [the bus]. Or, they would say, 'O.K., I have a little bit of time, so I'll go down to the corner, grab something [to eat] and come back,' but unfortunately, they wouldn't be going. Those were lessons that were kind of hard at the time, but it prepared you for everything, the interviews, the appointments, everything. I do what I have to do to make sure that I'm here on time. So, those are not only classroom lessons, but life lessons.

"There was a flight team at the school we attended [AATC] that would go to different aviation-related universities and compete. For example, they had a cross-country competition to see who would get there first, how much fuel they used, landing competitions—things like that. It was a moment for socializing and competing against other schools, and some of the guys were interested. They actually had a scheduled time for the meeting, but the time that was posted and the time that we were told were different from the actual time, so we showed up late. It was the same day, just different times. It only happened once. So we said, *You know what? We'll just do our own thing.*" This was Alabama in the 1990s, which wasn't that long ago, Wayne points out, but there were no blacks or women on the flight team at that time. "So we participated in the NAI [Negro Airmen's International] annual fly-in at Moton Field in Tuskegee, which allowed us to gain experience and build camaraderie.

"As we've gotten older," Wayne says in regard to his continued friendship with David D. Strachan, "our conversations have evolved and so you can dig deeper. Questions I've always wanted to ask, I'll ask him now and, you know, he's willing to answer them. We talk a lot about a lot of different things, not just flying. It's outside of that now, beyond that, so to speak."

Ewan Duncan

EWAN DUNCAN says he hadn't fully understood what a mentor was until he met David D. Strachan. "One of the key things that I would say is, in anything that you do in life, you need to have a mentor. You need to know that the person has actually walked the walk that you're trying to walk, has been there so they can show you the missteps not to take and how to get to where you need to be. And that's why you see the success rate of certain individuals vs. another set of individuals. It's because they have a mentor."

Ewan describes his life as "colorful," but his eyes begin to tear up when he talks about the ten years he spent in five different federal prisons. He was released in October 2010 and will finish his probation period in October 2015.

"What I enjoyed about Bro. Strachan, we not only learned how to fly, the theory and the practicality of it, but also how to manage our bank accounts, how to be respectful to one another, how to interact with one another, and who the enemy is as far as who's going to stop you from doing what you're trying to do. And none of us had this clue. We didn't hear this [at home]. Sometimes you have to be patient and understand: that's your brother or that's your sister. And that's how we addressed each other, brother and sister. Simple things. I address him as Bro. Strachan, my children say Bro. Strachan, my mom and dad call him Bro. Strachan. Both of my parents have a very good rapport with Bro. Strachan. He is, and I say this to him, like my adopted grandfather."

Ewan admits that all through high school he was a knucklehead. "My mother used to say, 'I'm going to call Bro. Strachan because he needs to talk to you.' I had the capacity to do other things, but the streets kept calling me." As a juvenile, he got himself into "a little bit nonsense" running around with the wrong crowd. He had applied to Brooklyn Tech for high school, but didn't get in because his application was late. "It so happened that Wingate was my zoned high school," Ewan says, but he did not find out about the aviation program at Wingate until his sophomore year. David D. Strachan reminded him of one of the teachers he had left behind in Jamaica. "They have a certain way they ran the classroom. There was no nonsense. You're there to learn, that's it. And Bro. Strachan was a serious, *serious* individual. He didn't play games. What he said was what it was; there was no gray area. He will give it to you, exactly what you're required to do, and if you do it, fine. If you don't do it, there's no in between. Later on, [if] you showed the tenacity and the drive, he'd make exceptions. I found that out in my junior year."

Both of Ewan's parents had worked for the government of Jamaica, his mom as a seamstress in the police and military uniform factory and his dad as a botanist. His dad also had a degree in the culinary arts and it was this latter trade that brought him to the United States as a baker. He eventually sponsored his wife and four kids: Ewan, one brother and two sisters.

Unfortunately for him, Ewan's parents bought a home in Yonkers, New York, part way through his high school years, but Ewan didn't want to change schools. "So I used to travel from Yonkers in Westchester County to Brooklyn, which is about a two-hour ride, to get to Wingate on time. And we had to be there prior to 7:00 a.m., fifteen minutes or so, when we went out to Farmingdale to fly, and I used to make that." Only once did Ewan have the bus door slammed in his face. "I wasn't angry, but I was like, 'This man is really serious.' No one laughed. We didn't ridicule each other that way because he let you have the opportunity to step back up, to redeem yourself, and this is why, even to this day, whenever he calls, whatever he asks for, I'm here one hundred percent. It's something that I can't describe, the things that he's done for me, *me*, personally. It's beyond anything."

After graduating in 1991, and having passed the Federal Aviation Administration (FAA) written exams for single-engine airplane, multi-engine airplane and certified flight instructor (CFI), Ewan attended Alabama Aviation and Technical College (AATC). He graduated in 1994 and came back to New York when he became a father. "At the time, I thought that was the best decision. My daughter was born in August, so I had to make a decision and I didn't consult with Bro. Strachan." In retrospect, Ewan now believes that David D. Strachan would have advised him to finish his education, regardless of his circumstances. "I was following what I saw my dad do, because when you're a dad, you take care of your family. I didn't know you could do both. I thought you had to give up one to fulfill the other. My parents didn't really interfere with my decision-making process; they thought I knew what I was doing."

In 1995, Ewan began working for the New York City Department of Environmental Protection (DEP). The co-parent of his child was working for Bell Atlantic at the time and all was well. A second child was born in 1998. "I was working and taking care of my family, but there was something amiss. I still kept in contact with the guys, so everyone knew [the situation] because I was very sociable. I wanted to stay motivated, but I also needed to maintain the foundation with my family and my responsibilities. Then, because I kept in touch, I spoke to Bro. Strachan. I said, 'Well, I'm here working for DEP and I'm trying to get back into the game, but…' At the time, I had not finished my bachelor's degree. This was 1999, and that's when I got the phone call."

Another Wingate pilot, Antonio Smith, was flight instructing at Moton Field in Tuskegee, Alabama, and he, too, was talking with David D. Strachan. He called Ewan to let him know about a flight instructor position at Moton Field. Ewan says that "all hell broke loose" vis-à-vis his family situation, but it was an opportunity to get back into aviation that he couldn't pass up. The person who ran the fixed-based operations (FBO) at the airport was Colonel Lewis, "another brother that actually helped to seed the progression of our success," says Ewan. Along with Antonio Smith and Bro. Strachan, "Colonel Lewis was instrumental in getting me back [in the game]. He's done a lot for the brothers. Never will I forget him. Colonel Lewis."

Ewan was elated by the opportunity. He and Antonio lived and worked at the airport while he made his re-entry into aviation. Then he got a call from another friend he had met while in Alabama the first time. "Really cool guy, very sharp-minded, but we were just on a different path." This person, who shall remain unnamed, was in the music industry and was in the market to buy an airplane to accommodate his travels. His recording studio was in Birmingham and he often had to attend concerts and recording sessions elsewhere. Ewan was able to broker a deal between this person and Colonel Lewis. As part of the deal, Ewan would be allowed to stay on as a flight instructor at Moton Field, but would fly for the unnamed employer on demand.

Once again, Ewan was overcome with joy. He was now earning a fairly decent salary *and* following his dream, teaching students to fly while also flying his new employer around the country. When his employer asked him to pick up something in Amarillo, Texas, he thought nothing of it. "I'd pick up the individual and he had luggage, no big deal, nothing alarming. Picked him up, dropped him off, came back to Atlanta, again, no big deal. Once, we flew out to Los Angeles for a fight and came back, but there was something wrong with the aircraft, so I had to bring it down to Amarillo to get it serviced. I went back to Amarillo to pick up the aircraft, but was unable to fly because of a sandstorm. So a guy came and delivered a couple of boxes. Again, no big deal. I loaded them up in the aircraft and flew back to Alabama."

In August 2000, Ewan flew via commercial airliner to California to visit his brother, Richard, who had just been accepted at a college there. When he disembarked to change flights at Los Angeles, he was met by two federal agents who initially said they wanted to ask him some questions.

"Bro. Strachan used to always say to us, 'Before you start answering any questions, find out exactly what the situation is. Find out if they are charging you with something.' They never did read me my rights. I didn't know how serious it was, and then they ushered me onto another aircraft and flew me to Texas. I called [my employer] and he got me an attorney. And he told me, 'Just relax, let me find out what's going on.' I made bond in Texas and left from there and came home to New York. I was scared to death."

It came out later that his employer was trafficking. Ewan was just one of many pawns that he used and was eventually convicted on the testimony of the person who had delivered the boxes in Amarillo. The fact that Ewan never knew what was in the boxes and never questioned his employer was irrelevant when it came to the law. "It was a bit of naiveté on my part because I didn't fully understand what was going on. He was someone I went to school with; I trusted him. I'd been flying and not paying any attention. I was so eager to get in the door because I'd been out of [aviation], and I just wanted to get back in."

Despite the situation, Ewan owns responsibility for his actions. "The law they said I broke was Code 841, criminal intent to distribute a manufactured substance, and Code 846, transporting illegal narcotics. I ended up getting 158 months, which is the equivalent of thirteen years in federal prison. I kept petitioning because I became a little bit savvier as far as how the law works and what I needed to do. Even though there was no physical evidence, because of that person's testimony I had to serve a mandatory minimum of ten years."

Filled with anger, frustration and pain, it took him a little while before he was able to talk to David D. Strachan. "I put Bro. Strachan's number on my calling list and I called him. He said, 'Where are you, brother? What's going on? I heard.' I told him I had been nervous and scared and I didn't know how he was going to react. So he says to me, 'Just tell me where you are. Do what you need to do and let me know when you've done it and I'll be there for you.' I was at Ft. Dix, New Jersey at the time and Bro. Strachan came to see me. He had just finished having surgery on his hips. Later, my dad brought him there and he came to see me on multiple occasions, but the very first time he came alone. Because he had metal in his hips, they wouldn't allow him in. He wanted to give them documentation, but they wouldn't take it. He had taken the bus to Ft. Dix and had to walk almost a mile from the front gate to the reception area. It upset me. It made me angry. Bro. Strachan is very passionate. He loves people, his family, his extended family, his friends, his community, and the brown skin. So Bro. Strachan said to me when he came back, 'What happened?' I said, 'I didn't know you were coming to see me.' He said, 'Brother, I would crawl on my belly under barbed wire to see you, if that's what it takes for you to stay motivated and to understand that someone really cares.' That's what he said to me…" Ewan's eyes tear up again and there is a long silence.

"My dad has really been an inspiration, and my mom, but just to understand what Bro. Strachan has given me. I speak to him quite often. He's guiding me through the maze of getting back to where I need to be, consistently being a mentor, consistently showing what unconditional love is for a person other than his own children. The same passion that I feel toward him is the way I feel toward all the brothers. I could go to their homes, be with their wives, their children, and not have an issue, other than like a brother to a sister, or an uncle to their children, that type of relationship. This is what he's established amongst us and how we view each other. I was ashamed when I went through my stuff, so that's why a lot of the brothers weren't able to come to my rescue. But there are brothers who've been through certain situations where the others are there, front and center, to make sure they have that support.

"There are issues that I have with my children and I call him and ask, 'Bro. Strachan, what do you think about this?' My eldest daughter is in college, at Penn State, right now. She's twenty. Everything that I get from him, I kind of relate back to them, even getting them to meet with Bro. Strachan because he has had such an impact on my life. It's something that I feel is important because of the sacrifice that he's made for *us*. I'm just hearing some of his stories now, because when we were kids, as students of Bro. Strachan in high school and also in Alabama, we weren't privy to some of the stuff that he's gone through. It wasn't until we became adults and now have families of our own [that] we're seeing all that. He has not changed since the very first time I met him, that's the truth."

Once again, Ewan is trying to get his life back and follow his dream. In December 2014, he finished his bachelor's degree at Empire State College. The federal rap will cost him some opportunities, but there are still options available to him such as flying privately or for corporations, or flying overseas. "Bro. Strachan is really big on working as a CFI here at home, so that's an option for me, but it's only through Bro. Strachan and the guys that it will happen."

In addition to stressing role models and mentors, Ewan also believes that those who have made it have an obligation to reach back and pull others forward. "Don't forget where you came from. Don't forget the people that you've passed along the way, who might be trying to do the same thing, or maybe not even the same thing, but trying to be successful. Don't forget to give them a hand. There's just so much that Bro. Strachan has done for me and the guys, but we also have a responsibility to Bro. Strachan and his legacy of being a fighter. We need to live that because we're not living for ourselves anymore. It's time now for us to give back."

Sitting in David D. Strachan's living room, Ewan says, "When I came home from prison in 2010, this is where I came and celebrated my freedom, in this house. My mom and my dad cried everyday while I was [in prison], worried what I was going through, but I knew I had this," and he points to the floor, "because I'd gotten it from him. And any prison I went to, no matter what the situation, I knew how to handle myself and I had that resilience because I understood the stuff that he's gone through. Even though I made a mistake, it doesn't mean I have to keep making mistakes. I can rise above that."

Ewan Duncan likes to tell everyone he meets about David D. Strachan. Someone once asked him, "Is he mythical?" Ewan responded with quiet reserve, "No, he's real."

Lester Tom

In a total pilot population of over 11,000, Captain LESTER TOM currently ranks as number 1,730 in seniority at United Airlines. He was hired by United Airlines in December 1988 and is currently a Boeing 777 captain. "When I upgraded to Boeing 737-300 captain in 1995, to my knowledge, I was at that time the youngest captain at United. I can't swear to it right now because of our merger with Continental Airlines, but I may be currently the youngest Boeing 777 captain at United." Lester is also type-rated on the B-767/757 and the Airbus 320. In addition to his ATP (Airline Transport Pilot) rating, he is also rated for Single Engine Seaplanes (SES) and is a Certified Flight Instructor for instrument/multi-engine aircraft (CFIIME).

Originally from the Republic of Trinidad and Tobago, Lester visited relatives in the United States for the first time when he was thirteen years old. "I came just for the summer, and then returned again at age fifteen to reside here permanently." That's when he met David D. Strachan.

Lester says that it was "a complete fluke" that he enrolled in a high school with a flight program. "My mother lived on Lefferts Avenue in Brooklyn a few blocks from Wingate High School. I was in the district, so that's the high school I attended. When I got there, there was another kid in line ahead of me at the registration desk. The person completing the registration process asked what he wanted to be when he grew up and he said, 'A pilot.' I remember thinking, 'This kid wants to be a pilot. *I* want to be a pilot,' and I remember sort of chuckling. He was told, 'Well, we have a flight program,' and that's when my ears perked up. I knew nothing of the aviation program when I came to register."

Lester was fortunate that day. Not only had the student ahead of him, whose name was Michael and with whom Lester became friends, broken the ice on the subject of piloting, but it was also the first year that Wingate H.S. was allowing ninth graders into the program. He was also fortunate in that the person at the desk gave him correct information. "Most of the staff, to my recollection, was Caucasian and most of the counselors, if not all, were Caucasian. I didn't always get good advice from counselors."

Lester entered Wingate as a freshman in 1981 and graduated a year and a half later in 1983. "I was in ninth grade at age fifteen and was quickly advanced to tenth grade, then to what's called tenth-grade advanced, [followed by] eleventh-grade advanced, and right into twelfth grade. By then, I had accumulated enough credits and completed the required citywide and Regents exams. I accomplished that by attending school early and taking a psychology course before most students came to school. For about a year, I skipped lunch and took a course. I also attended night school at a different high school and completed two or three classes there. I had a drive to complete high school as quickly as possible because I felt I had things to do and didn't want to spend any unnecessary time in high school. I was very much on a mission. Mr. Strachan's advice and guidance were pivotal."

Lester's mission was to become a pilot. "I've always had a fascination with airplanes," he says, "since I was six or seven years old." He describes himself as "one of those kids who couldn't let a plane fly overhead without looking outside to see what type it was." Although there was no one in his immediate family who was a pilot, he did have an older god-brother who was a captain at

British West Indies Airways (BWIA) who inspired him. Also, one of his aunts had a second home on the smaller island of Tobago and he would fly there often to help her with things around the house. "Often we would visit the cockpit, say 'hi' to the pilots, etc. I pretty much read everything that I could get my hands on that related to aviation.

"I would have flown one way or the other, with or without Mr. Strachan. I knew that was my destiny, to fly airplanes, but having a mentor like Mr. Strachan allowed me to develop into the pilot and person I am today. There's no way my career trajectory would have taken its path without Mr. Strachan's influence."

As a fifteen-year-old, Lester says he has to admit that he was a bit intimidated by David D. Strachan. "I personally felt that I had bitten off more than I could chew. When he described to us what to expect from the class, I thought, 'I don't think I'm up to this task.' But it soon became apparent that he was willing to work with you and do whatever it took to make sure you understood the material. He came across as disciplined, stern, task-oriented and maybe not very friendly. I can honestly tell you that that's not the case. He was always looking out for our best interests."

As an example, Lester describes the field trips to Republic Airport on Long Island. "We flew every week if the weather cooperated. To qualify to fly, we gave a presentation to our flight technology class. The topic could be related to any aircraft system or how to demonstrate a flight maneuver. The reason Mr. Strachan had us do this was because he didn't want us to go out there and be 'taken for a ride.' The City of New York was paying for our flying lessons through SUNY/Farmingdale. He didn't want instructors to take us up and just show us the sites. He wanted to make sure that we knew all the necessary procedures: pre-flight inspection, starting the engine, takeoff, turns, etc. He wanted to make sure that the instructors were teaching us the correct things. He made sure that we were well-prepared and knowledgeable."

Lester learned two major life lessons in David D. Strachan's classroom, to be persistent and to be prepared. "He had sayings he liked to give us. 'Preparation determines luck.' 'To be forewarned is to be forearmed.' Mr. Strachan prepared us to accomplish as much as we could in high school. Several of us completed our written exams before graduating, so when I was seventeen years old, I had completed my private, commercial and instrument pilot written exams." Lester explains that the youngest age at which a private pilot's license for a powered airplane can be obtained is seventeen years old. For a commercial pilot's license, the minimum age is eighteen. The written exam is good for a period of two years. "With Mr. Strachan's guidance, I passed those written exams before attending college."

In December 1983, he arrived at Alabama Aviation and Technical College (AATC). He quickly took his check rides and earned his private, commercial and instrument ratings; multi-engine rating; and single-engine flight instructor, multi-engine flight instructor and ground instructor ratings. While in Alabama, he also took courses through a nearby branch of Troy State University. (He eventually earned a B.A. in management leadership from Judson College, now Judson University.) He was hired by AATC as an instructor just prior to graduation and instructed there for a short period. He considered flying helicopters in the Army National Guard, but was involved in an automobile accident that changed his career path.

After his recovery, Lester discovered why David D. Strachan stressed perseverance to his students. "If I had given up at the first place where I was invited for a job interview and was rejected, I might be doing something else." He relates an incident that happened in the Carolinas with a company that had advertised pilot positions. "I spoke to them on the phone and gave them my background. They invited me to come for an interview. When I walked into the chief pilot's office, the same person I had spoken to, he saw me and in about ten seconds he said the job was taken."

Lester returned to New York in September 1985. "I started

flying aircraft for private individuals and also for members of NAI (Negro Airmen's International). After that, on the recommendation of an acquaintance, I headed to St. Thomas in the Virgin Islands and started flying DC-3's for Aero Virgin Islands Corp. I also flew for the lieutenant governor and several business people in St. Thomas. In addition, I operated a flight school for someone who become a very good friend."

Lester currently resides in a suburb of Chicago with his wife and three children. He says, "My success is Mr. Strachan's success. We'd like to think that we've done everything on our own, but nothing could be further from truth. The analogy of 'standing on the shoulders of those who have gone before you' gets misused many times, but certainly in this case, I am standing on the shoulders of many people, including Mr. Strachan, other pilots, of black people in general who have come before us and had the courage to clear a path. So the best I can do is to continue widening that path for others. My personal philosophy is, not just African Americans, but anybody who has the desire to fly, I will certainly attempt to help. Of course, there's a lot of pride involved when you help someone of African descent. Anything that we can do to improve our standing in aviation is a win for Mr. Strachan. That's something we will never forget: None of us would be where we are at this time in our lives, if it wasn't for him."

O'Neil Soares

O'NEIL SOARES met David D. Strachan through an outreach program that was sponsored by August Martin High School in Queens, New York. He says there are two words of advice he acquired from David D. Strachan that have helped him through his career over the years and that he will never forget: "Don't ever quit and don't believe anything *they* tell you."

A 1993 graduate of August Martin, which specializes in training students for aviation-related careers, O'Neil says that by the time he left high school he had acquired only 2.5 hours of flight time and hadn't taken any Federal Aviation Administration written exams for his pilot's licenses. He says he did not know anything about the aviation industry, what to expect, what the prerequisites were going to be to get a job, and most importantly, what the standards were by which he would be judged. The teachers and counselors at August Martin had told him nothing about state-funded aviation colleges and had steered him, along with other students, to private flight academies on Long Island or to the privately-run Embry-Riddle University in Florida. On his own, he had researched another flight school in Maryland. O'Neil says that the best part about meeting David D. Strachan was learning that he should get out of the Northeast.

"My direction totally changed. I was already on the path of aviation before I actually, physically met him, but I was in contact with him and he told me what I should do: Keep up my grades, where I should go, and the reasons why I should be leaving New York and going to Alabama. He told me about the other opportunities that were going to be available to me. He basically opened my eyes."

Armed with this information, O'Neil entered Alabama Aviation and Technical College (AATC) in November 1995, where he earned an A.A.S. in applied science and flight technology. After graduating, he stayed on as a flight instructor while going to school at night. After five years, he moved on to an airfreight outfitter in Vermont, Air Now, for a year before joining a regional airline, American Eagle, where he flew from 1999 to 2010. In 2010, he joined AirTran Airways as a first officer on the Boeing 717. That same year, AirTran was bought by Southwest Airlines. "I kept my date of hire, so I'm now in my sixth year at Southwest." In February 2015, O'Neil became a rated first officer on the Boeing 737.

In addition, O'Neil has served with the Air National Guard for the past eighteen years. He is currently a Tech Sergeant (E-6) with the 106th Rescue Wing out of Westhampton Beach, New York. In addition to his A.A.S. degree, O'Neil has an associate's degree in information technology from the Community College of the Air Force and a B.A. in management, which he earned in 1999 from Troy State University in Alabama.

A member of the Organization of Black Aerospace Professionals (OBAP), O'Neil says that black pilots are "scrutinized" more than others. "It was always harder. We're looked at in more detail. We have to be precise in everything that we've done.

"In the aviation industry, a lot depends on who you know, and we don't know all the players. We did not know people who could recommend us, but through the years that I was going through the training, speaking from Bro. Strachan's [perspective] of not accepting what they say [about us], never quitting—we did our studies, we got our flight time, we got our experience and book knowledge, and we knew, of course, what is what and how things work. So when we are actually tested, the way we pass, they cannot say that we don't know what we're doing. Once we get that recognition and a few of them get to fly with us, they see that we actually know our stuff, and that's where it kind of breaks down and we're accepted."

O'Neil has kept in contact with Bro. Strachan since high school and considers him an activist, a teacher, a counselor, and a father figure. "I have not been as regular as everyone else, but yes, I keep in touch, and he doesn't forget us. Bro. Strachan is awesome."

Anthony Robinson

One of the last students to have experienced David D. Strachan as a teacher at Wingate High School, ANTHONY ROBINSON graduated in 1993 and twenty-one years later, in May 2014, arrived at a major airline by way of Victoria's Secret. His progression through the maze exemplifies the network of support that David D. Strachan has created.

"Bro. Strachan was my flight technology teacher [through] twelfth grade. He was also my mentor in college. He was the one who recommended the flight school that a lot of us attended after Wingate, Alabama Aviation and Technical College (AATC). I got my private pilot's rating there, and also my commercial, instrument, multi-engine and instructor ratings. I instructed there for about two years. For a short period of time, I also instructed at Moton Field in Tuskegee, Alabama during the flight academies that were held there. Myself and Jim Bob Jones worked together with Colonel Lewis. In 2000, I left Alabama and came back to New York in pursuit of an airline career. They were hiring at the time. I [intended] to stay here for about a month, then head down to D.C. where I planned to instruct. That didn't work out, so I came back to New York. Up until 2006, I was working and getting my college degree. A lot of the brothers from AATC, Esan [Baptiste], O'Neil [Barnes], Vaslav Patterson, Leaford [Daley], kept calling me. 'Where are you?' they all asked, 'What are you waiting for? When are you getting back in?'"

Anthony remembers that September 11th kind of put a damper on things and that it was difficult to get a job, especially having been out of the industry so long. "Bro. Strachan always advised us, 'To get to the majors, you need to have a college degree.' And even talking with a lot of the brothers, it was the same message: You need to have some kind of degree. It doesn't necessarily have to be aviation-related, but you need something that shows you have dedicated yourself to a particular goal and you accomplished it. It says a lot.

"Anytime I came to a crossroad, I called Bro. Strachan and asked him for advice. Or I would get advised from brothers that were influenced by him. Sometimes you talked to [Anthony] Manswell, you talked to Esan [Baptiste]; it's like talking to Bro. Strachan. I had spoken to him about the decision to stay in New York and finish my degree. He gave me another option: I could pursue an online training course towards my degree while building up my hours. I know my personality. I know how I learn. Online training was not an option for me, so I told him that I would just walk away from the flying, put it on pause for a while and try to knock out the degree as quickly and as best as I could, and he said, 'That's fine. Just go with what works best for you.' So that's the avenue I chose. I stayed at home with my mom and went back to school. All the airlines require it, so I focused on getting my degree and that meant working during the day and going to school at night."

While earning his B.A. in computer information systems with a minor in business at Baruch College of the City University of New York (CUNY), Anthony "temped" during the day and in 2004 landed a job doing cost accounting at Victoria's Secret on Fifth Avenue. Working directly with managers and department heads just outside the offices of the CEO and CFO, he enjoyed many of the perks and benefits of being in a corporate headquarters. "I was having a lot of fun and doing really well, but I wasn't fulfilled because it wasn't that thing that drives me and I didn't really feel as if I belonged there. Everywhere I went, I would tell the story of how I used to fly. That was my passion."

Anthony remembers the exact moment when that passion had taken hold of him. He was seven years old on his way to visit his father in England. He had just received a toy airplane set, baggage loaders, cargo ramps and all, as a birthday gift from his father the previous spring. And after school, he would sometimes sit on the docks in Jamaica with his feet dangling toward the water, watching airplanes take off and land at Kingston Airport, always wondering where they were going. He was on the plane to London, coloring a fire engine with a bright red crayon, he remembers vividly, and contemplating becoming a fireman when one of the flight attendants invited him up to the cockpit to meet the captain. "There were three or four other boys and we all stood in line and waited to go into the cockpit. When it was my turn, I was immediately in awe of the whole experience. I walked in and saw the pilots in their white shirts and uniforms. The captain had his hat on and there was a first officer and a flight engineer. And then I looked around and there was a point where I saw past the pilots. It was as if they were not even in the space. All I could see were these beautiful cottony-white clouds kind of billowing in the most beautiful blue sky I'd ever seen. It was in that instant that I knew this was what I wanted to do. When I returned to Jamaica, I told my mother that I wanted to be a pilot."

His mother has always been extremely supportive of his career goal. "Nothing else mattered. All I ever spoke about and thought about was flying airplanes." Anthony was thirteen years old when they arrived in the United States in 1989 and entered junior high school in Brownsville about one-quarter of the way through the school year. His mother took the train on her days off to visit Aviation and August Martin High Schools in Queens, to talk to the teachers and find out more about the programs. Unfortunately, one of the requirements for getting into any of these specialty schools was that the student had to have four marking periods of grades, *i.e.*, a full school year. Despite the fact that he had straight A's, Anthony was not eligible to attend any of these schools because he had only three marking periods of grades.

Ironically, Anthony and his mother had met David D. Strachan at a high school recruiting event, but had ruled out Wingate because of it's bad reputation. "Bro. Strachan was there representing Wingate. He was telling us what it had to offer and he asked me what I wanted to do. I was a smart kid, but I was always very shy, so my mom said, 'He wants to fly airplanes.' And he said, 'Really? Not a lot of people know about it, but we have a really good aviation program at Wingate High School.' It was in that moment that Wingate started to sound a little better, but I didn't want to go to Wingate. I lived on East 91st St. in East Flatbush, so Wingate was a good twenty-five to thirty minute walk for me. He told us about the trips to the airport every Tuesday, all predicated upon your grades and your attendance. You'd have to get a permission slip signed by all your teachers, bring it to him and then, if everything checked out, you could go flying." Anthony was to learn that those permission slips were like gold. "Everybody wanted one of those slips. Many people fell by the wayside. Bro. Strachan always demanded that we keep our grade point averages up, or we weren't going to get a permission slip, and he meant it."

Anthony describes David D. Strachan as being loved and respected, "but he was also feared in a way where it's coming from a loving place because you don't want to disappoint him. You don't want him to be mad with you because you know you did something wrong. He's like a father figure in that sense. But at the same time, he's approachable. He gives you encouragement, he gives you information, and he has a way of opening your eyes to things that ordinarily you wouldn't think about before you got exposed to it. That way, you're prepared. He used to have this saying: *When the fool learns the game, the players have dispersed.* He'd write it on the board every morning when we came to class. It stuck with me."

It took Anthony a long time to understand what that saying meant. He recalls an analogy to a poker game that Mr. Strachan gave to illustrate the message in a different way. "If you're sitting down at the poker table and you're the new guy coming in, everybody else has been playing [together] for years and they kind of know each other, who cheats, and so forth. They tell you, 'Come on, sit down, you're one of us,' and they're slowly picking you apart and everybody's taking a piece. You're losing and [wondering], 'Why can't I win?' It's not until you have that *'Ah-ha!'* moment that you're being robbed that you realize you are the fool. Once you learn how things work, it's no longer fun for them anymore, so the game's over. The same thing happens in the corporate world and in the military. You try to rise in the ranks and you're wondering, 'Why am I knocking my head against these invisible walls and can't seem to break through?' and that's because of certain barriers that were put in place to hold you back. Once I got the message behind that saying, I began to see a lot of things more clearly and I also was able to bypass certain obstacles and understood things for what they really were."

Anthony demonstrates just how influential David D. Strachan has been in his life by revisiting a military career day that took place at JFK Airport. "Bro. Strachan told us about his military background and what happened to him. He kind of scared us away from going that route because he'd already done it." Nevertheless, a group from Wingate attended, himself, Burton Lumsden, another student named Chris, and several others from the class who eventually fell by the wayside and chose other careers. "Bro. Strachan huddled us into the corner and told us to look around at the military folks, what did we see. And we said, we see officers and workers. He said, 'All right, now what are the differences between who's in charge and who's not in charge? See if you can notice any common thread?' So we're walking around, some guys are wearing brown officer uniforms and some guys aren't. That still wasn't quite [what he wanted], but he asked questions, without telling us exactly what the end-goal was. We all started to get the picture that, a lot of times, those who are in charge were of a different tone than we were. We're not equal at all. They were in a commanding position, whereas we were always subordinate, the grunts, so to speak. And the lighter you are, the higher your earnings. As I moved on from that day, I started noticing that recurrent theme in different areas of my life.

"Bro. Strachan also taught us you can't blame others for all your problems. A lot of times, we're our own worst enemy and how we conduct ourselves in public says a lot. He says, 'You want to join corporate America. You want to be a pilot. You have to be a professional at all times. You have to look the part, you have to talk the part, you have to act the part.' He always demanded the best from us. We had to dress neatly, shirt tucked in, belt fastened, clean shoes, just look clean and presentable, no shirts hanging out and none of this flashy jewelry. We always looked the part and we were taught to be punctual. You have to respect people's time and if you're asked to be somewhere, you have to be there. It says a lot about you as a person. It says a lot about how you value yourself and how you value the opportunities that someone else is presenting you." Anthony admits that the lessons in punctuality were painful. More than once, he was left standing on the sidewalk as the bus to the airport pulled away.

So there he was in 2004 working at Victoria's Secret, making a good salary and having fun, "but the last year and a half or so, I started getting that itch to get back into flying full-time. Every time I saw an airplane flying over Central Park headed for Long Island, it took me back to the docks in Kingston when I was a child. One day I told one of the managers, 'Man, I miss flying.' In my mind, I knew what was going on, so that's when I decided to reach out to a friend in Florida, Christopher Rollins, who told me there were a lot of opportunities to get back into flying in that state just because of the sheer number of airports down there."

Anthony also contacted Burton Lumsden, his classmate from

Wingate who had taken over as flight technology teacher at Wingate High School after David D. Strachan's retirement. "We were in a lot of the same classes together and took the same trips to the airport with Bro. Strachan. I got in touch with Burton and went up with him whenever there was an opening. I'd get in an hour or two of flying, just to build up some time and get proficient. Once that happened, I also sought out an examiner for my flight instructor certificate, which had expired. I took the CFI [Certified Flight Instructor] course in New Jersey and I also had to do the recurrent ground training out in Islip, Long Island." It took Anthony about a year to get current and then, in the spring of 2006, he obtained a buddy pass from another one of his Wingate classmates, Anthony Hunter, who was flying for a major airline. He flew down to Florida to explore the opportunities Christopher had told him about. "I had this longing in my gut that said, 'This is what I want to do if I'm ever going to be happy with myself down the road.' I'd been out of it for six years at that point."

In September 2006, with no definite job prospects, no place to live, and about $1500 in savings, Anthony put in his resignation at Victoria's Secret and three days later was on his way to Florida. "All I had was a wing and a prayer, but I told myself I'd give myself two years to get back into the industry, give it my all, and really make a go of it. If it was God's will for me, then so be it. If not, then I could carry on with the rest of my life with whatever endeavors I decided to do, knowing that I had tried. I didn't just walk away from it. I didn't just quit."

Christopher helped him shop out his résumé to all the companies doing business at Ft. Lauderdale Executive Airport. Ironically, Christopher, who had graduated from Wingate after Anthony, had been one of his flight students at AATC. Another Wingate student, Kenworth Booth, rented him a room. "I got to Ft. Lauderdale on a Friday night, about ten o'clock and I met with this guy. I was wondering why the name sounded familiar. He looked at me and said, 'You know, we know each other.' Turns out he was also in

Bro. Strachan's flight technology class. His family had moved to Ft. Lauderdale midway through high school and Kenworth finished high school in Florida." At that point, Anthony and Kenworth had not seen each other in more than fifteen years!

Things moved quickly once he arrived in Ft. Lauderdale. By July 2007, Anthony was flying with SkyWest, a regional airline on the West Coast. On Memorial Day 2014, he got word from JetBlue Airlines that he had just been hired. "For years, 99.99% of the decisions we've made regarding our careers have all been under the counsel of Bro. Strachan. My mother spoke to Bro. Strachan even when I was in high school. From [Anthony] Manswell on down to the guys after me, we have all reached back and said, 'Hey, Bro. Strachan, this is what I'm dealing with. I'm having this issue with this particular person in this situation.' We were all in contact with [Anthony] Manswell and this is why I say that, even though there were times when I was not talking with Bro. Strachan directly, he was always a phone call away."

Jahvon Tuitt

At the end of the 1995 school year, JAHVON TUITT flew from his island home of Montserrat in the British West Indies to visit his father in Brooklyn, New York, just as he had done every summer since 1989. He looked forward to their annual shopping trip for new clothes and school supplies to take back with him in September, but this year was different. In June, the volcano that is the island of Montserrat erupted for the first time in four hundred years. By September, three-quarters of the island was uninhabitable and the remainder of the island was being evacuated.

Stranded in Brooklyn, Jahvon and his father had to quickly apply for a change in status for Jahvon's visa and enroll him in school. On the district border between Boys' and Girls' and Wingate High Schools, his father preferred Boys' and Girls' because of the disciplinarian reputation of the principal there. Mr. Mickens was notorious for chasing drug dealers away from the school with a baseball bat. Nevertheless, father and son wanted to check both options, and discovered upon visiting the guidance office at Wingate that the Elijah McCoy Academy, the engineering department at Wingate H.S. that was named after the African American inventor of the automatic coupling system (the "Real" McCoy), contained a flight technology program. The deal was sealed.

"I will never forget my first day at Wingate," Jahvon says. "It was October 31$^{st}$ and I was egged at the door." Wearing fresh new black jeans, Jahvon was not fazed. He knew what to expect of American schools, he thought, from the television program, *Saved by the Bell*. After a visit to the bathroom to clean up the mess, Jahvon reported to his first class. Shortly thereafter, he came face-to-face with David D. Strachan.

In vivid detail, Jahvon recollects his experiences going through the flight technology program at Wingate H.S. "My teacher was Mr. Guy Belgrave. He had been one of Mr. Strachan's students also and came back to Wingate to teach. We introduced [ourselves] and then Mr. Strachan came into the classroom and introduced himself to us. He asked questions and we'd give him back an answer and he would say, 'Oh, you're a smarty-smart.' I got that ominous title from Day One."

Apparently, David D. Strachan's first lesson in life for Jahvon Tuitt concerned the facts about what ingredients go into a hot dog. "It was just how Mr. Strachan introduced himself. He was definitely about telling us what we can do, as men and women of color. It wasn't only about engineering; he gave us a cultural history. Remember, we had African Americans and Caribbean students in the class and for some reason, we feel that we're so different, but Mr. Strachan would say, 'You really have to understand that you are perceived in this world by one spectrum, and you must think that way in order to get through it.' He told us how he used to fly crop dusters in the South and that we needed to really respect the [flight] program and get as much out of it as possible because so much was put into it, that we could not take it for granted." Jahvon adds, "There we were in Crown Heights on the border of Flatbush, black students learning how to fly: unheard of!

"Mr. Strachan reminded me of my old schoolmaster back in the Caribbean, somebody you *had to* respect because he would not settle for less. He expected you to do well even if you didn't think you could, and he brought you up to his level; he opened up your potential. 'Mediocrity' is just another word that he knows. Everybody knew that whenever Mr. Belgrave was not there, Mr. Strachan was going to come in and it wasn't going to be a situation where you could make noise or jump around. He would review the chapter and then he would give us lessons in life. He would ask us questions and he would tell us how it was in Alabama, the experiences that he had in the 1950s, and it was interesting because I'm a historian. It was a unique opportunity to actually be able to ask a question and get a direct response."

Jahvon recalls that not all of the students appreciated Mr. Strachan's no-nonsense approach, "But hindsight is definitely 20/20," he says, "because he was being that way only because he realized that you have to set the rules properly. Students at that time had so many distractions and time is something that you can never get back. His approach to some may have seemed a little harsh, but I wouldn't change him, I would not change Mr. Strachan one bit! He knew exactly what to say; he knew exactly what you needed to hear at that time. The funny thing about it, even if you knew he was right, you wouldn't tell him. You wouldn't want to give him the satisfaction of knowing that he was right, but you knew for a fact that he was."

With even more enthusiasm and detail, Jahvon describes the weekly procedure for going out to Farmingdale, Long Island to fly. "The way in which you were selected to go to the airport was based on your grades. 'Nothing is given to you in this world, especially as people of color,' Mr. Strachan would say. 'You have to earn it and you have to work hard for it.' Only the top scorers on tests would get the slots because he had a certain amount of slots per semester and a certain amount of money in the budget. From the outset, you were supposed to achieve academically in order to get this benefit. We would learn the theory in class and the practical we'd learn at Republic Airport every Tuesday. Mr. Strachan demanded that you dressed the part. You had to wear a shirt and tie. In the summer, he would allow us to wear a polo shirt. I never tied a tie in my life until that time. I would have to wake my father up at four o'clock in the morning to tie my tie.

"We'd meet in the lobby of Wingate H.S. around five o'clock in the morning and we'd wait for the big yellow cheese bus to come. Mr. Strachan's habit was to sit behind the guard desk and we'd all line up. We signed out our cushions (I was short and I couldn't see over the yoke), our headsets, and if you had a fuel testing tube, you'd bring that with you. And you had your checklist and your clipboard. We all lined up along the rail and he would be there reading something, and we'd wait. We knew what was coming. He would always want to occupy the time, so he'd say, 'All right, it's not a joyride. You have to know what you're doing when you get out there.' So he would call you, 'Mr. Tuitt, what's VX? What's VY? What do you do under these circumstances?' Mr. Strachan would call you out randomly and *God forbid* you didn't know because he would [say], 'Wait a minute. Do you know the opportunity you have here? How could you not know this?' Mind you, this was the top tier of students. Then you made sure, the next time he called you, you knew what it was.

"We'd file out to the bus, but you wanted to be on line for that bus because Mr. Strachan sat on the right hand side of the driver. And you didn't want to be in the first, second or third seat behind him because when we hit [the highway], he would get up and turn around and if you were in his line-of-fire, you were going to get the next [question]. So everybody made a beeline to the back of the bus. He would walk up and down the aisle and you'd still get a question, but nobody wanted to be there in the spotlight for the first question. He would ask questions and you'd be going through your procedures, and when you finally got it, you [whispered], 'Thank you,' because you'd survived this round. Then he would sit down again."

Once they arrived at the airport, Jahvon remembers, "The instructors would normally be there waiting for us and [Mr. Strachan] would pair us up. [One student] would fly from Farmingdale to Brookhaven or Waterbury or some other place, and then you'd switch and the other student would fly back." In this manner, each student actually received two lessons per flight, says Jahvon.

"And when we had parent-teacher nights, he'd come out in the hallway and he knew everybody in the flight program. He would have to make a comment about you [to your parents]. If you got a pleasant comment from Mr. Strachan, you were on top of the world because to get that is worth its weight in gold. He would not beat around the bush. He would say to your parents, 'This guy is too distracted,' and so forth. He was very, very honest, so if you got a compliment from Mr. Strachan, it was prized more than other teachers' because you knew the other teachers might sugar-coat. Not Mr. Strachan, and that is why I treasure his friendship right now." Jahvon says that David D. Strachan has had a major impact on his way of thinking. "There are certain people who make benchmarks in your life. He is definitely one of them.

"When you think about Mr. Strachan, you run through your mind the different scenarios that we had in high school and you realize how time has proven him right. And you think, 'It's a good thing that Mr. Strachan was there to tell me this, or to say that, or to give me this guidance.' And you don't want to lose contact," says Jahvon. But he did lose contact for a while. He was actually able to conjure up the phone number by recalling how it had been written on the weekly permission slips for the trip to the airport. He tried the number from memory and when Mr. Strachan answered the phone, he immediately recognized Jahvon's voice as his "smarty-smart."

Jahvon soloed at Republic Airport, but never got his pilot's license. After graduating from Wingate in 1999 with a 90+ average, he received a full scholarship offer from the Spartan College of Aeronautics and Technology in Tulsa, Oklahoma and also an offer of scholarship assistance from Embry-Riddle University in Florida, but both of these financial aid packages were tied to federal funds, thus making him ineligible. "I was in this gray box called 'temporary protected status' because of the volcano. There was a backlog in the immigration situation and in order to accept the federal dollars, I had to be a resident or a citizen." Alabama Aviation and Technical College was also off-limits because of expense; without residency, he did not qualify for student loans.

It took eight years for Jahvon to cut through the red tape and adjust his status. In the interim, he was able to qualify for several private and community-level scholarships and to attend City College of the City University of New York for two and a half years, majoring in political science and Caribbean history. He expects to finish his B.A. in June 2015. Working full-time as a member of the ground crew for a major carrier at JFK Airport, he plans to obtain his pilot's license and continue flying, but only as a hobby. "I still have my logbook and everything," he says. He hopes to combine his love of flying, his interest in politics and his loyalty to his country into one fulfilling career. He's not certain how he's going to do that, but he's confident that, living on a tiny island with a volcano, having a pilot's license will be an advantage.

Jahvon talks about how David D. Strachan has helped him in his evolution beyond the field of aviation. "Coming from Montserrat, which is still a British colony, we're very anglicized. We celebrate British holidays and we grow up in this British shadow of how things [are] supposed to be done. Everything is order. Wearing jeans to church was near heresy and when I came to the United States and saw people doing that, I frowned at them because [at home] you had to wear your Sunday best. That's the term. And when I went to City College, it *radicalized* me. It opened up my mind to such different ways of thinking away from the British way of thinking. When I would talk to Mr. Strachan, I always had the benefit of being able to say, 'This is what happened at college today,' and he would give me another [point of view] and we would speak about it. Mr. Strachan is a very direct person."

Jahvon thinks of Mr. Strachan as his mentor. "Anything that I need to discuss—politics, life, school, *anything*—Mr. Strachan is always there. Sometimes when I'm walking through Bed-Stuy

[Bedford-Stuyvesant, a neighborhood in Brooklyn] or when I'm on the A-train, I'll just call him and he will recommend books for me to read. It's like high school all over again when I would think I knew something and he would listen, and then scold me after and send me to do my homework. He's very adept at what he does and he's very up-to-date with what's going on. He was disappointed, of course, when I finished high school and couldn't do the pilot [training], but he put me onto WBAI, to *Democracy Now* with Amy Goodman, to all of these astute political thinkers that I would listen to during the whole up and down of the Bush years with the hanging chads, the election, the war in Iraq and how it was perceived, everything. I was listening to all of these people, and me and Mr. Strachan would call each other and fifteen minutes could turn into three hours."

Franklin Rodriguez

My name is FRANKLIN RODRIGUEZ and for me, knowing Bro. Strachan has definitely helped me. When I took the path towards becoming a pilot, he made that path a little bit clearer. I knew that I wanted to become a pilot when I left George Washington High School in uptown Manhattan (Washington Heights), but my grades when I graduated weren't that great. I was not an ideal student. I had applied to several colleges and the only college with an aviation program that accepted me was SUNY/Farmingdale on Long Island. I was still lost in terms of what direction I was actually going to be taking in this career.

My school friend Enrique Ballenilla met Bro. Strachan on the flight line one day and came back and told me all about him. Ever since that early morning, Bro. Strachan has been advising us, giving us information as far as where to go for the best training and what to do along the way. On his advice, Enrique went to an aviation school in Alabama. After graduating a year later, I followed. By then I had been to Bro. Strachan's house where he spoke with me in his unique paternal way. He instilled in me that if this was the path I really wanted to take, that I should take the necessary steps, go to Alabama Aviation and Technical College (AATC), and get all my certificates and ratings and all the flying experience required. Flight training there was extremely affordable and Bro. Strachan was always a phone call away. Foreseeing that AATC was only a two-year school, Bro. Strachan insisted that we find a four-year school where a bachelor's degree would then make us eligible to join the Air National Guard as a flight crew officer. To this day, I still remember doing mock interviews in his living room for the position in the Air National Guard, a practice that gave me an edge over the other candidates who had butterflies in their stomachs while waiting to be seen.

As a captain in the New York Air National Guard, I flew the largest cargo aircraft in the U.S. military fleet, the C-5A, for seven years (1998-2005). Then I made a mistake, for which I take full responsibility and for which I am now serving time in a federal prison. I stay in contact with Bro. Strachan by telephone and via regular mail, and I am planning a reunion with him when I am released in 2017.

Bro. Strachan has always been my main mentor in life. He always said that, being that we are people of color, we have to strive not just to be the same, but to be better. That always resonated with me. During my college years, I strived not just to have a passing grade or a passing performance, but to really excel. It's kind of hard now saying all this because of the circumstances in which I find myself, but there is a lesson to be learned in everything. Bro. Strachan is like a father in respect to teaching us how to become a better person. He's humble, paternal with the guys and girls he is helping, and a true altruist.

My advice to young people who aspire to be pilots would be to stay on the straight path and never let anybody tell you that you can't do something. If your dream is to become a pilot, whether it's a commercial airline pilot, corporate pilot, or an astronaut, just stay true to your dream until you have accomplished it. Nothing is impossible. I never really thought my dream would take me as far as it did.

To David D. Strachan I say this: Thank you for caring with such a beautiful heart and an uplifting spirit. I look forward to one day giving back to the youth just as much as you have given me. You will forever be the father who counseled me, the big brother I never had, and a friend who anybody would be profoundly grateful to have.

Franklin Rodriguez

Marlon Rankine

Even though he attended Wingate High School in Brooklyn, MAR-LON RANKINE knew nothing about the flight program at Wingate until after he'd graduated. "I was talking to one of my high school friends just by chance," he says. "An airplane flew over and I said, 'Man, what I wouldn't do to be able to do that,' and my friend said, 'How come you weren't in the flight program?' I said, 'What flight program?' Marlon had told his guidance counselor, whose name he remembers quite well because she was also his homeroom teacher, what his aspirations were from the very beginning. "I've always wanted to be a pilot. This lady never once mentioned the flight program to me. Here was a person who knew clearly what I wanted to do and told me to try and get a job at Brooklyn Union Gas as a meter reader, and she even set up an interview for me. I was in the same building with David D. Strachan for three years and didn't even know he was there. It was just by chance that I happened to be with this fellow who went to Wingate, too. He didn't want to be a pilot, but he actually had Bro. Strachan's telephone number." Marlon doesn't remember the young man's name, but he took the phone number and called David D. Strachan. "That was the best day of my life. Bro. Strachan and I have been in touch since I was eighteen years old."

Says Marlon, who lives in a suburb of Atlanta, "Here I am now, a licensed commercial pilot and flying anything I want. I have an MBA and I'm an entrepreneur. I left New York City in 1989 to get flight training and I have never spent more than seventy-two hours there since I left." He remembers the NYC public school system as "an intellectual wasteland for black people" and strongly believes that people like his guidance counselor should be in prison, "because they've done this to a lot of people... Bro. Strachan used to tell me, 'Always know who your enemy is,' and I'm sure others got that same advice. He also used to say, 'When the fool learns the game, the players have dispersed.' Any black man in America who shows up to get pilot training—I'm not talking about a private pilot's license; it's not like anybody cares about that—when you start trying to get a commercial pilot's license, when you start trying to get the ratings that are going to pay you money and take you all over the world, that's when it gets to be very dangerous."

Marlon received some of his flight training at Alabama Aviation and Technical College and some at Delaware State University. "Alabama was Bro. Strachan's recommendation because they were offering flight training very cheaply, but that's all you got, the flight training. I realized I needed a four-year degree, so I ended up going to Delaware State where I was able to get a B.S. *and* the flight training. A black man without an education is going nowhere."

Following Bro. Strachan's recommendation, Marlon also took the Air Force Officer Qualifying Test (AFOQT) and did well, but in the end made the decision not to seek a commission in the Air National Guard. "In those days, the Guard advertised pilot slots just like any other job, with the promise that they would train successful candidates to fly. Keep in mind, I was already a pilot when I took the test and at that point I had my four-year degree as well, so I was completely qualified. I went through interviews and it was amazing to listen to all the excuses I heard like, 'Your flying experience isn't current.' *As opposed to what?* Somebody who's never even been behind the controls of an airplane? You're going to train someone who's never flown, but not someone who's already qualified? And this is the foolishness that I was hearing from these people. If I hadn't had someone like Bro. Strachan who forewarned me that this is what goes on, I probably would have been completely demoralized when I came up against this." After much interviewing and more excuses, Marlon decided that he was not going to put his life on the line for such foolishness.

"Black people don't know what it is they're dealing with, and a lot of it is because they don't have a Bro. Strachan in their lives. I would even go so far as to say that, for most people, the window of opportunity to really get them moving in the right direction is probably up to about 25 years old. After that, it becomes increasingly difficult just to keep up." According to Marlon, black pilots make up less than one per cent of all people who fly airplanes commercially, including corporations, airlines and even crop dusters, "because you have to have a commercial pilot's license to do that, too."

Marlon says that a lot of David D. Strachan's students didn't make it. "We were, in my opinion, like the Tuskegee Airmen. That was a completely different time, a completely different situation, but a lot of what they were faced with, we were faced with, too. A lot of the challenges were the same because the mentality of white people hasn't changed much since WWII." He describes David D. Strachan as inspirational, a realist, very pragmatic, and someone who is *beyond* intelligent. "I can't even say intelligent because you have plenty of intelligent fools out there. He's very knowledgeable, but not only does he have all this information, he knows how to put it to use for practical purposes to achieve ends, which a lot of people can't do."

At the same time, Marlon "blames" David D. Strachan for why he is still single. "Bro. Strachan taught me what to look for in people and how to decide what type of person I needed in my life to help me succeed. Following his advice has been difficult, it has been inconvenient, but it has kept me out of divorce court and when I look at people who [marry for the wrong reasons] just because they don't know any better, their lives are a living hell."

Born in the United States, Marlon went to Jamaica when he was two months old and came back to the U.S. when it was time to start school. He is looking for ways to combine his love of flying with his business, possibly doing aerial surveying for people who own large tracts of land or who are otherwise involved in the real estate industry. He admits that he is at a crossroads: he wants to be an aviator, but the entrepreneurial side of him wants to experiment and see what happens. "I'm still thinking of flying, but there's something else that keeps me interested." He also considers the possibility of flying overseas. "I wanted to leave the U.S. years ago. The only reason I didn't is because a little girl came along. My daughter is now thirteen."

Marlon says he talks to Bro. Strachan on a regular basis about these issues and more.

"[Flying] is something that for a lot of different reasons is going to continue to be marketable, at least for the rest of my lifetime, just because of what's going on in the world with aviation, geopolitics, the global economy—all of these different pieces that have nothing to do with Bro. Strachan." Nevertheless, he says, if it were not for David D. Strachan, he would not be in possession of this highly marketable skill. "Bro. Strachan challenged me to be a better person. He knows this road that you're on; he's been on it… Every white person I talked to discouraged me. One told me, 'You can't be a pilot because you wear glasses.' Another one told me, 'You're too short.' I've heard all kinds of nonsense. These people are in positions of authority. They have the ability to shape the thoughts of young people and that's why young people get discouraged. Bro. Strachan understood this and shared this same power as well. And no matter what they did, they weren't going to take that power from him."

Neal Hagley

My name is NEAL HAGLEY and I was a student of David D. Strachan's at Wingate High School in Brooklyn, New York, from 1980 to 1982. He's very fair, and I would add insightful, and from the day I met him my life changed.

I was born in Grenada and I came to the United States in 1979. If you know anything about the education system in the Caribbean versus the U.S., it is totally different, so my first year at Wingate was, to be frank, boring. I was not being challenged and a lot of times I would not even go to class. I felt like, "Why am I here? I can do all this stuff." Toward the end of the first year, and I recall this vividly, I was leaving the cafeteria and I walked by Mr. Strachan's classroom. He had a little balsam model airplane in his hand and I'm standing there looking at this airplane and I was mesmerized. His door was open, so I walked into the room. He obviously didn't know me. I introduced myself and I asked him, "What is this class really about?" He says, "Well, it prepares you, if you're interested, for a career in aviation, or learning to be a pilot. Would you like to do this?" And I said, "Are you kidding me?" So I'm standing there and I can't believe it.

I have no recollection of guidance counselors at Wingate H.S. sitting down with me and laying out the programs or explaining that there was a flight program. They created this program, but they never expected it to work because they didn't know what our potential was. He took something that was designed for kids to have fun and keep them out of trouble, turned it around and created pilots from it. In my opinion, he single-handedly did it all by himself. I remember going home that day and telling my mom that I'd met this man and there was a flight program, that I was going to try this program, at least for a few months, and she kind of humored me and said, "O.K., all right, I believe you."

I came back to school in September and started the flight program. The first time I took a flight was on November 9, 1980, and I remember it was interesting, but what was ironic about it was that I'd been waiting to do this for so long, but when I flew the first time, I got really, really sick. The second time I got sick and the third time I got sick. I'm thinking, "Wait a second, maybe I should try something else." So I went to Mr. Strachan one day after school. We talked about it for a while and he said, "Is this what you want to do?" I said, "Yeah, but I'm really concerned about it." He said, "Well, you aren't the only person this has happened to. You've just got to keep going and keep plugging away. You never know what you're capable of." Mr. Strachan was a motivator. He cares about humanity and he let's you know you can accomplish anything you want. His gift is to take someone and have them live up to their own expectations, or what they're capable of being. That, I think, is his greatest gift.

He used to always say to us, and I remember this very well. We would be in flight class and he would say, "You know, not all of you will be pilots. Not all of you will want to be pilots. Even though this is an aviation class," he'd say, "my goal here is to let you know, regardless of where you come from or what your background is, you're capable of doing anything. As you go through life, as you face challenges in life, regardless of what those challenges are, failure is not an option."

I'll tell you an interesting story: I started flying in 1980, and most people don't realize this, but at the time we were in a really bad recession. All the airlines were laying people off and here I am, sixteen years old and I'm telling people that I'm going to be a pilot. People were saying, "Oh, come on, it's going to be too hard to get a job. No one can get hired right now." I remember talking to Mr. Strachan about this one day and he looked at me and said, "Five years from now, if the airlines decide they're going to hire one pilot, why couldn't that one pilot be you?" And I was stunned by what he'd said. Let's be frank: There's a race issue here and it's extreme because you had black pilots from WWII and the Korean War who couldn't find work and they were hiring these white pilots with *zero* experience and paying for their training. I always say that the biggest gift I received from Mr. Strachan was not how to become a pilot; the biggest gift I received from him was learning how to navigate the challenges of life and still be a good citizen, still be a respectful individual, and still be able to perform in the society in which we live in. That, I think, was his biggest gift.

I am currently the captain on the Airbus-320 at United Airlines. I still have my job, but I'm actually on leave right now because of health issues. As a black pilot, especially as a black captain, you are constantly under scrutiny. They are always watching you, even your co-workers whom you, in theory, supervise. My first year at United, every time I would come to work, the captain would ask me, "What's your background? Where have you been before? What have you done?" And the irony is, most of us they had hired at that time—me, Anthony Manswell, Lester Tom, Andrew Cummings—had more experience than these captains when they were hired several years prior. We live in society as black people and because of the society, we have health issues, we have other issues, and it's a lot for us to deal with. At this moment, I haven't flown an airplane in over two years, but I live my life, regardless of what I'm dealing with, and I always refer to what Mr. Strachan told us: "Remain positive, and if you want something badly enough, there's nothing you can't accomplish." And I teach my kids the same thing. I don't care what you do, whether you want to be a doctor, a lawyer, whatever, but whatever you do, do the best you can and if you fail, that's O.K. At least you tried.

It's an amazing story, it really is, and it needs to be told.

Neal Hagley

Anthony Hunter

ANTHONY HUNTER recalls one time at Wingate High School when he tried to cheat on a test in Mr. Strachan's flight technology class. "It was part of the pilot's written exam and I decided I was going to cheat because I couldn't bother studying. I was too busy doing everything else. So the test day comes and I have my cheat sheet under the test. He's sitting over there doing his thing and he has his head down, looking at a book or something. He gets up and walks over to me. He walks behind me. And then he says, 'Brother, let me see how you're doing on the test.' He pulls my paper," and Anthony demonstrates the abrupt motion, "and the cheat sheet did a somersault in front of me and fell on the ground. I'm visibly shaking now because I'm thinking, 'I'm done. I'm going to get thrown out of the program. I'm going to have to figure out how to do this on my own.' You know what Bro. Strachan did? He didn't touch the cheat sheet. He just put my paper back on my desk and walked away, sat at his desk, and put his head down again. He never said a word to me about it. Up to this day, he has never mentioned it. Really, if he had said anything to me, I was going to tell him, 'Bro. Strachan, you told me, *By any means necessary.* Did you not mean it?' That's what I was going to say to him. But he never said a word. I failed that test because I didn't have my cheat sheet. I sat there shaking for the whole period because I thought that was the end for me, that he was going to come down on me 'like a ton of bricks' as he always used to say, and he never did. Most teachers would have tossed me out of the class, but he's a master at psychology. He gets into your head and he makes you do things you don't want to do, and like it, not knowing that you like it. That's how good he was. Ever since that day, I've told myself the easiest way to cheat is to put the information here," he says, pointing to his head.

Years later, that lesson came back to him as he consistently earned 90s and 100s in a college class where he would finish tests in 15-20 minutes. The professor asked him directly if he was cheating and he told him no. "So how do you finish so fast?" the professor wanted to know. Anthony told him, "I studied."

Anthony says that he and some of his fellow students in the flight program had a name for David D. Strachan: *The Enforcer*. "He was very compassionate, energetic, dedicated, and he didn't take any slack from us at all. He didn't give us an inch. His favorite words for us were, 'I'm going to come down on you like a ton of bricks if you don't follow my instructions.' It wasn't that he was going to hurt us, or anything like that. He had, I think, over all of us a kind of mental control like a father and a son. The son recognizes that the father is in charge and, whether you want to resist him or not, you find yourself unable to because he's the father figure that you tend to want to follow. Not only was he forceful with us so far as making sure we did our lessons, but he was caring."

Anthony had started the program in ninth grade with a different teacher. "That teacher wasn't very knowledgeable, but we thought he was. We didn't know any better. Or, at least, he didn't impart any of his knowledge to us. It *was* a flight technology class and [we all wanted] very much to become pilots, but all he talked about was maintenance. I think I spent maybe one year with this guy and as time went on, the only thing we were left knowing was how to look at an airplane engine. He didn't teach us anything about flight. Later on, after he was fired, we learned that he had told the principal, 'I don't expect them to be pilots, anyway.' Here is somebody who is responsible for educating us in the subject he's hired to teach and he says, 'I don't expect them to be pilots.' I'm not saying he said it because he was European; he said it because he looked at us and saw no future and he wasn't interested in providing one, which is the exact reason he's there, to provide a future to his students."

In tenth grade, Anthony met David D. Strachan for the first time. "Before I met him, a lot of the guys were saying that he was a racist. They would said, 'He's always talking about how Europeans are trying to take this from us, take that from us,' but none of those guys are here today. None of them are within our group and some of them are not alive. Some of them dismissed him because, when we got him as a teacher, he made sure that all of us had the truth about life, the hard truth. He used to tell us, 'The most feared black man in America is an educated one,' but he wasn't making racial slurs. He was telling you the truth. As a kid growing up, you didn't hear this stuff and mentally, you were expected to fail. As a child you probably told yourself, 'I'm not going to make it, anyway. I live in this neighborhood, I go to this school.' So, after a few months in his class, I realized what everybody was saying about him wasn't true. He's pro-black as opposed to being *anti-* any other race. You couldn't dispute what he was saying, the facts. He always told us, 'Go learn your history. If you don't know your history, then you don't know yourself.'

"I was kind of a stubborn teenager, one of those that refused to give in. I was like, 'He's not going to push me around. No way. I'm not giving in.' So, I would intentionally try to resist him and I wouldn't get trip-slips to go to the airport. If you didn't perform well in class the week before, you wouldn't get a trip-slip, and because I was being stubborn, he recognized that. He didn't push me; I guess he figured if he pushed me, he was going to lose me, so he kind of allowed me to make my own mistakes, and when I didn't get a trip-slip, he would say, 'Brother, you didn't perform. You didn't do what you're supposed to do, so you can't be rewarded.' No violin overture. Some of the other guys achieved their private pilot licenses in high school. I didn't come close because I was the rebel."

Anthony remembers that he always came to flight technology class late because it was his first period class and he walked to school. "One day, he said to me, 'Bro. Hunter, why are you always late to class?'" He and Mr. Strachan talked about his lateness for a moment and Anthony started thinking, "This guy is getting me now. He's going to come down on me. My butt is in trouble," but instead, Mr. Strachan started asking him questions. The ensuing discussion focused on citizenship and the opportunities—scholarships, government jobs, etc.—that would become available to Anthony if he became a U.S. citizen. "As a kid, I had no interest in this stuff. That was way ahead of me. I hadn't thought that far, but I listened to him and I realized, here's this guy, always threatening to punish me for something, but he took the time to really get into my mind and figure out, 'Who are you and why are you doing this? Cause this is not helping you. Let me show you another way.'

"This was a different side of Mr. Strachan because I was used to The Enforcer. He wouldn't let me in the classroom, but he took me outside and talked to me in the hallway and after that, I don't know, something clicked. The lights came on, and ever since then my grades in his class went through the roof. Things changed for me. I'd always wanted to fly ever since I was a child. You find most pilots are like that. They've always had a bug that you can't get rid of. I used to make airplanes out of beach bottles. I would take a bottle, tie cardboard to it, cut the sides of the cardboard, tie a string to it, and spin it around with a propeller on the front. I'd destroy all my toys, take the engines out and make airplanes. One day, my grandfather and I were sitting out in the yard in Jamaica, looking up at the sky and he said, 'What are you looking at there?' I said, 'The airplane.' And then I said, 'Grandfather, one day I'm going to be a pilot.' I was maybe eight or nine years old at the time and he said, 'Well, go! That's a good goal to shoot for.' But I never knew how to do it, and up until that time when Mr. Strachan talked to me outside the classroom, I still didn't know how to do it. I was in the class, but I was thinking, 'I've got to figure this out because I'm coming close to graduation and I still don't have a plan.'"

Anthony remembers that perhaps thirty to forty minutes of Mr. Strachan's class wasn't about the lesson. "It was about life and how you should handle yourself as a black man in this country. How you should approach your lessons. How you should approach manhood. How you should act on the weekends when you go out. He'd say, 'Brother, don't be standing on the side of the road when you have nothing to do so the police [can] come by and knock you upside your head and drag you off to jail.' Because of that, as a teenager growing up, I never hung out. Nobody else said this to me, and I had a mother and a father I grew up with, but my parents would tell me don't get into trouble, without details. He'd tell us, 'Come over here. Look at those knuckleheads out there on the corner. They should be in class. The police are going to come by and they're going to jail.' He would repeat this constantly, so you're hearing it all the time, and it makes you think about what you want to do with your life.

"During high school, we didn't know Bro. Strachan as anybody but an educator. We called him Mr. Strachan. We didn't know the person inside of him. He never shared any of that with us. It wasn't until we got to college, sitting around, talking, that questions began to emerge. What happened to his wife? Where are his kids? Over the years, he would share more. A friend of mine, Ewan Duncan—he lived across the street from me [at college]—he and I reminisce a lot about it. We think about the things that went on in Mr. Strachan's classroom, and then we started to notice a pattern, the progression of the man himself, getting an insight into who he is and the way he started treating us differently. As students," Anthony says, "there was a very clear relationship, the lines were drawn and you knew where you were. As we got older, now we're becoming men and the fruits of his labor are flourishing and you can see that [he was thinking], 'I don't have to push these guys anymore. They're doing it on their own, and they're pushing others.' I rebelled against everything and if he hadn't pushed me, pushed a lot of us, I can speak for myself and say I probably wouldn't be flying an airplane at an airline. I didn't know how to get there. I didn't have a plan."

Anthony graduated from Wingate in 1990 and joined his classmates at Alabama Aviation and Technical College (AATC) in 1992. He recalls that Alabama, as a young black adult, was not a place for him. "We used to run around the school for exercise, a three-mile run, and people would drive by and shout the N-word at us sometimes, but it would just roll off our backs because Bro. Strachan had prepared us for it. It was shocking, and that's why I said those life lessons really helped us, at least, they really helped me because when things like that would happen, I wouldn't freak out. I wouldn't get angry because I would think back to what Bro. Strachan said and he always told us, 'There's a fight you can win and there's one you can't, but you have to think about it,' and I know that if I go over there and punch that guy in the nose and start a fight, I'm not going to win. And when 'The Law' gets involved, that's even worse. You're lucky if you end up in jail. Those life lessons really prepared me, so when it happened, I knew how to handle it. I also knew why they were doing it. They hated us because they were shortsighted and it's something they've learned since they were this high. They don't even know why they're doing it. It's like Pavlov's theory: You clap your hands, you get a response. So, I didn't let it affect me. And because of that, I learned how to excel. I graduated six months early, but I had to stay there for the other six months because I didn't quite finish the flying. I still had some check rides to do, but as far as the academics, I was done."

After graduating from AATC in 1994, Anthony went to St. Francis College in downtown Brooklyn while simultaneously working at a bank. He started out as an aviation science major, but ended up with a B.A. in aviation administration because of an all-too-familiar administrative mistake with his courses. "They made me take classes I wasn't supposed to take. I thought I was going to graduate and then I hear, 'No, you didn't complete the required courses.' So I went to the Dean and he said, 'The only thing we can do is change your major. That would reduce your requirements and include some of the classes you already took.' And that's how I came to switch." After graduating from St. Francis, Anthony landed a position as a flight instructor at Teeterboro Airport in New Jersey. From there he went to Chattaqua Airlines, a regional carrier serving New York State, and from there he was hired by Continental Airlines and has been at United Airlines ever since the merger with Continental in 2010.

With a loud sigh, Anthony describes how he responds to the everyday challenges of being a black man in what is unfortunately considered a white man's domain. "Even walking through the airport, sometimes you can see the displeasure in some of the passengers' faces when they see me in uniform. It's very common." He tells a story about a woman who mistook him for a porter one time while he was passing through the terminal on his way to the plane. "I got out of the car, I'm in full uniform. I was a captain at the time, so I had my captain's wreath on my hat, my luggage, and this lady, she was European, she looks at me and says, 'Here are my bags. Could you take them to the guy over there?' I looked her right in the eye and leaned in really close and whispered, 'The Redcap is over there,' and I waited for her eyes to move and then she had to think about it. I walked away and left her standing there with a stupid look on her face. I like to do that to them. Being angry isn't going to solve any problems. I don't get angry because in their hearts I know they're so angry. You walk around with that much anger all the time and it's going to eat you alive. So there's nothing I can do to make what you're doing to yourself any worse. That is comfort to my mind." Anthony says that he would not know how to handle any of this had it not been for Bro. Strachan. "I would not be prepared for what really happens to a black man in this country. And a lot of these young black boys are not prepared. They don't know how to deal with the anger."

Anthony Hunter is now a first officer on the Boeing 757/767 and says that, in his mind, he can always hear Bro. Strachan saying, 'I'm gonna come down on you like a ton of bricks,' but he laughs when he thinks about it. "When we were in college, we would always go over to Tuskegee and judge the fly-ins at Moton Field. Bro. Strachan came down a couple of times and at that point, he stopped treating us like students. He would always treat us with high regard and he would just sit back and stare at us and smile. That's because, without him, a lot of us wouldn't be here. I'm not going to say 'all' because I can't be that definitive about it, but a lot of us. He never chastised us for decisions we made. Never! A lot of guys were afraid to call him when they screwed up. I called him and said, 'I screwed up,' and he said, 'Don't worry about it. Everybody does. You'll be bouncing back soon. This is what I can do for you. Call this guy…' and he was ready to help, all the time. He never, ever turned us away when we were in need. He never judged us. Never!"

Sheldon Hewitt

SHELDON HEWITT is not only a successful commercial pilot, he's a story-teller *par excellence*. "It's always a pleasure to talk about Mr. Strachan," he begins. "This man personally changed the lives of, I can't count the exact number, but anywhere between a hundred and two hundred pilots, and a majority of us are flying at major airlines. The interesting thing is we're all together. That's how our network [works] because of Mr. Strachan: no one goes anywhere and you have to worry about him. This is what this man did for us. This was a game-changer."

Sheldon credits the Tuskegee Airmen International (TAI), the Organization of black Aerospace Professionals (OBAP), and the Negro Airmen International (NAI) with helping to spread the word about "Mr. Strachan's program," and helping him and others move up through the ranks. "I totally walk in the shadow of the Tuskegee Airmen. Things that they did broke down a lot of barriers for us. That said, there have also been some challenges. For example, going to certain individuals to try to get the information and figure out how to go about becoming successful. That was missing. Mr. Strachan filled that gap, despite what he went through in the military. It's great that the Tuskegee Airmen accomplished what they did, but there was no pathway for the rest of us to flow through. You didn't have the roadmap, you didn't know how to get there. Mr. Strachan did all of this. He didn't have to do it. He could have just sat back, taught school, got all his ratings, and just gone on with his day-to-day life. So, I mean, I could talk for hours…" And he does.

"For me, the path has been fairly smooth, but it's been smooth because of timing and because of all the information that I got from all the folks that, once again, came out of Mr. Strachan's program at Wingate High School. Anthony [Manswell] was a first lieutenant when I went down to Alabama Aviation and Technical College (AATC). He used to bring the A-10 down to AATC just for us. That's a game-changer, too. The barriers that Tony broke down going through the Air National Guard, the hiring wave at United, all those things, I'm standing on those guys' shoulders. So there was a pathway for me. I had options compared to prior folks. They had to experience a lot of things that I didn't have to experience because they went first."

Sheldon has been flying the Boeing 757/767 (two different aircraft with similar systems and therefore one type rating) with UPS since April 2005. "Anything is possible, but it would have been much more of a challenge [to get here] and I probably wouldn't have been here at the age that I am, without the information and the roadmap that Mr. Strachan laid out. I probably would have made it to the airlines…probably in [my] fifties and only had fifteen years left of airline time. Mr. Strachan cut the red tape out of that. He told us, 'This is what you need to do, get it done, and that's it.'"

Sheldon's mother wanted him to become a doctor, but he was rejected by Hillcrest High School in New York City, where he would have prepared for a career in medicine. He learned from a junior high school friend, O'Neil Soares, that August Martin High School in Queens had a flight program. Sheldon applied and was accepted. He remembers two individuals, both of them African American, who came to the school and spoke to students in the flight program. The first was a flight engineer at the now-defunct

TWA, a gentleman in his late forties or early fifties. "He told us some of the paths he took to get into aviation and it seemed like his path took a very long time. But when Mr. Strachan came to the school, I thought, this man has something different about what he's trying to get across to us here. And [I wondered] why is he taking his own time to come here and do this? There were students who questioned Mr. Strachan, guys in the class who said, 'Why should I listen to you? Why should I even trust you? Where's your proof? Where are your facts?' Questions." Sheldon says it was the way the information was presented, compared to the other gentleman's, that made him sit up and take notice. "Information is the key to power and success, correct information. You can't make a decision without the correct information. And that's what this is all about. It's not lack of motivation. It's lack of information."

After graduating from high school, Sheldon took a year off from flying and worked as an automotive mechanic. "My last two years in high school were not the greatest, and on top of it, I found something that I liked, working on cars. I like fixing things." He'd been slightly discouraged from becoming a pilot by the flight instructors on Long Island who, he believes, were trying to steer black students away from aviation careers. "They would talk to you like you were an idiot and do things, like 'Hey, you want to see a pencil float?' and put the airplane in a negative-G [gravity] dive, which kind of scares you out of the intention of flying. When I was going through, there weren't any African American or Latino [instructors], or female. So, it became very challenging at that time and I asked myself, 'Do I really want to do this?'" Almost a year later, he ran into his friend O'Neil in the mall. "He had just come back from Alabama and he had his private pilot's license. I said, *What?!* Right after that, I spoke to Dick Burbank at AATC and I packed my bags."

At AATC, Sheldon met his lifelong friends, now members of the support network that was created by David D. Strachan. His roommate, Jermaine Robinson; Wayne Brown; Leroy Kinlocke, who, Sheldon remembers, "was like the spider web in the center keeping everyone together while we were at AATC"; Michael White, who's now an airplane mechanic; Esan Baptiste, and many others. "There was a whole group of folks that you just fit into and you found support. You didn't have to worry about how you're going to make it through this process, coming all the way from New York, away from your family, down to Alabama. And even though it was 1994, the racial divide was still there, but you had these guys that were already established and because of the pipeline that started with Tony Manswell, all of that made a difference for us to flow through there. Andrew [Cummings] did not attend AATC, but he was a part of the process, too, and Willis [Reid] out in Oklahoma.

"And believe it or not, two individuals messed up, but that's another thing about our group of guys and being around Mr. Strachan. Normally, most people, when somebody messes up in life, they throw him under the bus. They don't want to have anything to do with him. Not when you're in Mr. Strachan's camp," Sheldon emphasizes. He talks at length about his relationship with Franklin Rodriguez, how they were flight instructors together, how Franklin had shown him a few things when he went into the Air National Guard. "It was a very challenging time, but it doesn't mean we throw him away. People make mistakes. No one is perfect. I had my issues in the Guard. When I came back from training, I told Mr. Strachan what happened. You know what his comment was? 'Well, brother, one door closes, another one opens up.' As soon as he said that, I got a call from this company and they hired me. So how do you put a price tag on anything like that?"

Sheldon says that finding an affordable college was a challenge. "That's why Alabama was the perfect location. AATC had a great training program. It was about an hour and a half from Tuskegee, so you had that environment to keep you motivated, and you had a great training environment at Fort Rucker where you could go and fly [with the military]. Three different approaches, all within an hour to an hour and a half, which means saving quite a lot of money when you're talking about flight time that you've got to pay for. All these things made a tremendous difference." Sheldon says they knew about the racial barriers in Alabama, but that their priority was finding a place with inexpensive flight time that was not hard to get to. "We could have gone all the way out to Arizona, but that's halfway across the U.S., so airline tickets, things of that nature, would have been a challenge. I don't know how Mr. Strachan and Tony Manswell came up with it, but they took a lot of these things into consideration and it all came together. It was perfect.

"The year after I got to Alabama, that's when I reconnected with Mr. Strachan. We got really close. He told me a lot of great things, a lot of good information. Even before I took my AFOQT [Air Force Officer's Qualification Test], I had a great understanding from Mr. Strachan. And he says, 'Listen, when you go into these environments, you have to be prepared. There are folks who don't want you to be there. They're uncomfortable because you're young and you're black.' And I get that even now because I'm forty years old and I was hired when I was thirty. I get folks that'll use comments like 'Oh, sure, well you're a baby,' and I know where it's coming from. Most of them have gotten hired in their twenties and thirties, but we do it, it's a different story."

Sheldon graduated from AATC and worked as a flight instructor for two years while finishing his B.S. degree in management at Troy State University and trying to get into the Air National Guard. "I did have a short stint with the Guard out of Stewart AFB in Newburgh, New York, the 105th Air Wing, but it didn't work out for me. The goal with the military was that you didn't want to go into the Air Force without knowing anything about airplanes, because you didn't want to get washed out. You want to have some type of knowledge of how they were going to train you. The second thing is, you wanted to be an officer because you didn't want to go into some enlisted rank and they tell you, Hey, aviation is not for you, the same thing that they did with Mr. Strachan when he was in the Air Force." Sheldon opted to get out of the Guard and almost immediately was hired by a cargo outfitter, Air Now, where he flew for approximately six months. In 2000, he moved up to a commuter airline, Atlantic Coast Airlines, out of Washington, D.C. and flew with them until 2005.

Sheldon tells a story second-hand to illustrate some of the tactics that are designed to discourage black youth and make them give up their pursuit of a career as a professional pilot. "When it comes to training, Charles [Tai] takes his training very, very seriously. Apparently, Charles had graduated from AATC and was finishing up his undergraduate degree in New York City. He went out to Long Island with a group of friends to take the AFOQT, which is part of the recruitment process into the Air National Guard. The results came back and the master sergeant who [administered] the test told Charles he didn't meet the criteria. Charles questioned the statement, 'didn't meet the criteria' and was told that he had failed the test. Charles called Anthony [Manswell] and Anthony asked him what his scores were. Charles was like, 'I don't know, they told me I didn't pass.' Anthony hung up the phone and called a master sergeant he knew in Washington, D.C. She brought up the scores and said, 'Oh, yeah, this guy not only passed, these scores are fighter pilot scores.' So, that was a game-changer for Charles. He would not be in the Air Force if he had given up. The fact of the matter is, you need the numbers. You have to verify all the information. Never take anything for granted because you don't know what other people's motives or intentions are. That was just another career [that] could have been railroaded. Thank goodness Charles had an Anthony Manswell who had the understanding and the discipline to make sure that everything was correct. That came from Mr. Strachan.

"It's not just in aviation [that] Mr. Strachan had an impact on us. It's everything, our whole well-being. For example, the last few years he's had some health issues and he's gone to a more holistic approach. He passed that on to us: 'This is why you have to eat right. This is what you have to do to keep yourself in shape, not just to be healthy as a pilot, but also to be on this Earth for quite a longer time.' That's the thing about Mr. Strachan. It's a holistic approach to everything, our finances, trying to get your life in order, things of that nature. When you're screwing up, he'll tell you you're screwing up. That's what you want. You never want a person that only tells you what you want to hear. And that's why I *love* Mr. Strachan," Sheldon says, stressing the word 'love.' "When you know someone just generally cares about his guys, making sure that we're successful and that our families are successful, and that the other folks who come behind us are successful, whatever endeavor you've taken on, it's phenomenal."

Sheldon says that he has come across many folks who didn't really understand David D. Strachan. "You have to understand the man. His story has not been told because he's a very private, serious person. He's not looking for any accolades. Unfortunately, in this industry, guys like to walk around with a high chest and [mouth] off about their accomplishments. Well, what have they really accomplished? What are they doing to change [things] like the changes that Mr. Strachan made, like some of the Tuskegee Airmen made? It's not to say, 'Well, we're pilots and now we can just walk around and get all this respect.' It's not about respect. It's about what Tony [Manswell] did, the amount of people that [have] gotten hired under his tutelage over at United. Some folks who took the information never even came back and said thank you. And the problem is, we have a lot of folks who went a different path and don't know anything about Mr. Strachan and how he helped a significant amount of folks. When we talk about blacks in aviation or in any professional ranks, we see a few folks and we think everything is great now. There are still a lot of issues that are preventing people from reaching their full potential."

Although Sheldon has never personally had to be involved in any legal action to obtain a flying position, he fully recognizes the fact that he is standing on the shoulders of those who have. He cites the 1960s lawsuit against Continental Airlines. "Thanks to

Mr. Strachan and Tony and other individuals like Marlon Green, we understood the reason we needed a footprint to make sure that we go where we need to go. You want to be a pilot? This is the path you need to take so you can get there at an early age and enjoy seniority, and so that there's no missteps in the process."

One of Sheldon's primary concerns about the future is that the pipeline that was created by David D. Strachan no longer exists. "Not only are the young people not getting the information, but the other problem is trying to find out who the motivated young students are. [We] had August Martin High School, where Mr. Strachan could come to; [we] had Wingate. The enthusiasm that we had, compared to the enthusiasm of the kids that are out there today, that's the biggest problem, especially since we are in a social-media frenzy. The information should be a lot easier [to access], but it's not. I keep using the word 'game-changer' because there's no telling how many of us may have been caught up in the [justice] system; that's the reality when you don't motivate kids in any community. That made a huge difference. And how much money was spent to do that between the 1980s and 1990s? [The amount] is so small for how much we have gained. The whole purpose of why we spend tax dollars is to try to improve the quality of life so that folks are independent and can stand on their own two feet. That's what this program did."

Sheldon remembers not having a lot of money when he first came back to New York from Alabama. "Times were real hard and I was going through interviews for the Air National Guard. Before I had my first interview, I had no clue about what I needed to wear, the type of suit, tie, shoes, etc. Mr. Strachan took me to Manhattan and said, 'We have to get you a Brooks Brothers shirt, some wing-tipped shoes, etc.' He told me that I had to have a high-powered tie, one that represented how I viewed the United States. How your hair is cut, all those things made a difference in my interview. And when I came up short [of money], he said, 'I got it.' There are just so many [things] that Mr. Strachan has done for all of us, and that's why I call him a game-changer. I was just watching Charles Rangel, the representative from New York, on television and he had his challenges going through the military, too. That's what needs to be explained, what Mr. Strachan went through and what he did. That's what this whole story, in my opinion, is about."

Charles Tai

Born in New York of Jamaican parents, CHARLES TAI graduated from Park West High School in Manhattan, a 35-40 minute
subway ride from his home every morning and afternoon, even
though he lived "just up the hill" from Wingate High School in
Brooklyn. Even though he had been interested in aviation as a
child growing up in the streets of Brooklyn, and despite the fact
that his older brother had attended Wingate, no one in his junior
high school had informed him of the flight technology program
right there in his own neighborhood. On the advice of a teacher at
Park West, he attended Embry-Riddle Aeronautical University in
Daytona Beach, Florida after graduation, believing that he could
not go wrong at what was considered the "Ivy League" of flight
schools. "I was [supposed] to get my degree there, as well as my
commercial, multi-engine and instrument ratings, but the cost of
tuition and flying fees were expensive. I had to leave after about a
year and a half."

In December of 1989, Andrew Cummings, a Wingate pilot
who was also a good friend of the Tai family in Brooklyn, told
Charles to call David D. Strachan, and he did. It was on the advice
of Mr. Strachan that he eventually transferred to Alabama Aviation
and Technical College (AATC). "I took a trip down to Alabama
in the beginning of 1990 and when I went there, it was like being

back in Brooklyn again! Everyone was from my neighborhood, so I felt like I was back home." Anthony Manswell, another Wingate pilot, introduced him to the concept of the Air National Guard. A third Wingate pilot, the late Leroy Kinlocke, invited him to a reunion at Wingate H.S. after graduation from AATC, and that is when Charles finally met David D. Strachan face-to-face.

"What I really respect about him is he's very upfront. He doesn't hold anything back. He puts it as it is. He says there are going to be people out there who are going to attempt to hold you back. They don't want you to be in the position that you're in, so they'll do whatever they can to prevent you from getting into that position. And even if you do get into that position, they're going to try and make your life difficult."

Charles Tai holds the rank of lieutenant colonel in the New Jersey Air National Guard_and in the footsteps of other Wingate pilots, has recently joined United Airlines.

Garfield Graham

My name is GARFIELD GRAHAM and I will start with saying that I feel very lucky to have met Brother Strachan back at Wingate High School. I was enrolled in the aviation class almost by accident. I wasn't certain what I wanted to become in life, but after spending some time in his class and learning about other young men like myself who became professional pilots, I quickly knew that I could also become a pilot. I recall riding on the bus from Wingate to Long Island with Brother Strachan, on our way to the airport where we got flight lessons, and he would give us his speech. He gave me the knowledge and inspired me with the confidence to deal with the obstructions that would be in my way when I began my career in aviation. He also gave me step-by-step information on which aviation college to apply to, what forms to fill out for financial aid, and so forth. So I have to give him credit for where I am today. From a poor family in Brooklyn, with Brother Strachan's early direction, I was able to stay out of trouble and now I have achieved the position of captain on the Airbus 330 and 340 aircraft out of Dubai. If I were to name one person to whom to attribute my success, it would be Brother Strachan.

As Brother Strachan used to say, those *turkeys* don't want me sitting there next to them as a pilot. They don't consider me their equal. He told us, "Work hard at your goal, become good at your craft." In my experience, I have had to prove myself in the cock-pit and in the simulators all the time. In many cases, I've had to become better than my peers in training, being one of the few or in some cases the only minority in the group. Hard work and resilience is the reason why many of us are still in the business. I have had doors closed in my face whilst looking for opportunities and the same has happened to some of my friends in aviation, but resilience and hard work keeps us going, as many give up the fight when things get rough.

Sorry it took so long to get back to you with my few words. I just finished up my recurrent training yesterday, which was quite rigorous, and later today I will be heading down to Tanzania.

Garfield Graham
December 2014

Kendrick Antoine

My name is KENDRICK ANTOINE and I have to say that becoming a professional pilot was not my initial plan as a teenager. Fortunately, my interest in computer technology was thwarted by city high school zoning laws. Discovering the aviation program at Wingate High School was purely accidental, which led to meeting the most influential person in my entire life, Mr. David Strachan.

Mr. Strachan has been and continues to be a beacon of light and pillar of strength and motivation to me, as well as to several hundred others. He has been responsible for providing me with the knowledge that prepared me for an aviation career specifically, but also for life in general. Mr. Strachan did not teach classroom subjects only. He taught us how to conduct ourselves in a world filled with traps, for people of color especially. I really don't know where I would be or in what state if I had not met Mr. Strachan. I can say that he has been a father figure in many ways where my own father was not experienced. David Strachan has shown care and compassion and given guidance, encouragement, direction, and motivation to my life.

I am here today because of Mr. Strachan. What he has given to me is immeasurable and can never be repaid in kind to him, but I know he has not and never will look for repayment. His reward and happiness is seeing the effectiveness of his contribution to my being successful in absorbing and applying his guidance today. He is a true role model in my life. Instead of just giving me a fish, Mr. Strachan taught me how to fish. I highly commend Mr. Strachan on being able to accomplish all he has without much external help, if any. His early life may not have gone exactly as he planned, but David Strachan turned his misfortunes around and passed on his experiences to me so that I would not encounter the same in my journey through life. That is the ultimate selflessness, for which I will never be able to thank him enough.

Kendrick Antoine

# Afterword

This is a story of personal transformation, from my near self-esteem death in white-supremacist America of the 1950s while in the Air Force pilot training program in Bainbridge, Georgia, and from family tragedy in Nashville, Tennessee, to later successes of my black students who many saw through a lens of low-to-no expectations. Those students defied all barriers and went on to become professional airline and military pilots. This is *my* victory.

I feel compelled to talk to my students about the value of the Wingate High School flight class experience. My students hit the jackpot by being in my class. Teaching was my love and my passion, and my mission has always been that of empowering other human beings. This in no way takes away from the positive experiences you've had elsewhere, including support from your families in achieving your goal of being a pilot. I say to all Wingate pilots that many others have had the dream of being a pilot with much family support, but they didn't make it because they were not in the right place at the right time, as you were. They did not have the good fortune to be at Wingate to get the training and knowledge that you got in my class. Never let amnesia allow you to forget the huge advantage that you were blessed with by being one of my students at Wingate High School. Always remember, as you take the captain's seat, that there are many others who are just as smart as you are, who never got the opportunity that you were given.

There is great value for people of color who want to be pilots joining or creating a network of the like-minded who can identify, support and empower one another in achieving the goal of being a pilot. Don't be a lone wolf, if you can avoid it. Your enemy will always find it easier to pick you off when you do not have a support system in your life.

# Acknowledgements

With much love and gratitude, I would like to acknowledge my partner, Monica Rose, who encouraged me to write this book and supported me throughout the entire project, and the brilliant editor, Brenda Carpenter, whose fantastic work brought this project to fruition.

I would also like to acknowledge my brother, Edward A. Strachan, for his help gathering materials for this book and for his support all along; my cousins, Ivy Parks and Clarice Donaldson, who have been very supportive and helpful to me in raising my family and researching the family tree; my son, David, Jr., and my daughters, Davia Strachan Rosemond and Dina Dawn Strachan; my friends Fay Bennett Lord, Victoria Robinson and Phyllis Andrews, for encouraging me to write this memoir; and my best friend in life, the late Leo Downes, the source of endless wisdom that he shared with me.

A huge measure of gratitude goes to Gary Geoghegan, without whose initial technical assistance this project would have never gotten off the ground, and to Tim Sheard of Hard Ball Press for his guidance in bringing this story to print; to my students, both pilots and non-pilots alike, without whose successes my life would have been that much emptier: *they empowered me*; to Reevaluation Counseling and the Lifespring Program, which helped me heal from the tragedies that took place early in my life; and to the Rev. Dr. Eric Butterworth of Unity Church, the same source of inspiration tapped by the poet, Maya Angelou, and who empowered me spiritually with positive self-worth and values that I could then share with my students.

I would also like to recognize Francine, the owner of the coffee shop on Malcolm X Blvd. around the corner from my house in Brooklyn, who thought so much of my accomplishments that she would correct visitors who dared to call me by my first name!

All of these individuals have added to the richness of my life and made this memoir possible.

D.D.S.

Proof

Made in the USA
Charleston, SC
31 August 2015